TILL MURDER DO US PART

For a complete list of books, visit JamesPatterson.com.

TILL MURDER DO US PART

TRUE-CRIME THRILLERS

JAMES PATTERSON

WITH ANDREW BOURELLE AND MAX DiLALLO

As Seen on

INVESTIGATION DISCOVERY

GRAND CENTRAL PUBLISHING

NEW YORK BOSTON

The crimes in this book are 100 percent real. Certain elements of the stories, some scenes and dialogue, locations, names, and characters have been fictionalized, but these stories are about real people committing real crimes, with real, horrifying consequences.

Grand Central Publishing
Hachette Book Group
1290 Avenue of the Americas, New York, NY 10104
grandcentralpublishing.com
twitter.com/grandcentralpub

Originally published in trade paperback and ebook in January 2021
First oversize mass market edition: December 2021

Grand Central Publishing is a division of Hachette Book Group, Inc. The Grand Central Publishing name and logo is a trademark of Hachette Book Group, Inc.

ISBNs: 9781538752524 (oversize mass market), 9781538752494 (ebook)

Printed in the United States of America

OPM

10 9 8 7 6 5 4 3 2 1

TILL MURDER DO US PART 1
James Patterson with Andrew Bourelle

RAMP UP TO MURDER 197
James Patterson with Max DiLallo

TILL MURDER DO US PART

JAMES PATTERSON

WITH ANDREW BOURELLE

PROLOGUE

San Joaquin County, California
August 7, 1980

FRIENDS REGGIE SANDERS and Pat Moorehouse walk along a path parallel to a concrete channel filled with slow-moving water. There isn't a cloud in the sky, and the sun reflects off the steel-gray surface, making visibility into the water impossible. Between them, the two men are carrying fishing poles, tackle boxes, portable lawn chairs, and a small cooler. The cooler currently contains only a six-pack of Schlitz, though the men hope it will be full of striped bass when they make this walk in reverse in a few hours.

"Are we there yet?" Pat asks, his forehead beaded with sweat.

"Almost," Reggie assures him. "It's just up here. I'm telling you—I saw all kinds of fish in there. You won't be sorry."

A few weeks ago, Reggie and his wife had taken an evening walk along the canal, and he'd spotted a section where dozens of fish were swimming. The deeper water is nearly opaque, but in the right light, the top foot or so is translucent enough to allow for glimpsing what's floating around down there. As soon as Reggie saw how many fish there were, he told Pat they needed to come throw some lines in and try to land a few—though it's taken the men, who both work at the nearby Altamont Speedway, until now to find time in their schedules to go fishing.

The waterway—technically named the Governor Edmund G. Brown California Aqueduct, though most people simply call it the California Aqueduct—is a series of canals and tunnels carrying water throughout the state. Its four hundred miles of waterways also happen to be full of fish, at least in this twenty-foot-wide section outside the city of Tracy.

It's morning, but the temperature is already warm. The day is only going to get hotter, so the two friends will probably knock off by early afternoon. There isn't any shade out here.

"Here it is," Reggie says. "The spot I was telling you about."

He sets down his tackle box and lawn chair, and takes the teardrop-shaped fishing net dangling from his belt and drops it in the dirt.

"I don't see any," Pat says, squinting down at the water. It's hard to see anything because of the angle of the sun reflecting brightly off the surface. "You said the water was so thick with them that you could practically walk across it."

"That was a figure of speech," Reggie says.

The men set up their lawn chairs and open their tackle boxes. Reggie has also brought a Styrofoam container of live night crawlers, and the two men bait their hooks with squirming worms and then cast their lines out into the water.

"Want a beer?" Pat asks.

"Does the pope shit in the woods?" Reggie laughs

as Pat tosses him a Schlitz. "It's nice and quiet out here, ain't it?"

"Sure is."

It's hard to believe that to the east, the bustling San Francisco Bay Area is not far away. But here, among the beige sandy walkways along the canal and the fields of golden hay stretching in all directions, the crowded metropolitan world feels very distant.

"Hey," Pat says, sitting up in his chair and pulling on his pole. "I think I got one."

His rod curves sharply as he tries to reel in whatever is on the end of the line.

"Nah," he says, disappointed. "It ain't no fish. I'm snagged on something."

"Huh," Reggie says. "Wonder what it could be."

One benefit of fishing in the aqueduct is that it's relatively free of debris. Compared to a river or lake, there are few logs, branches, and rocks. Snagging a hook on something is relatively uncommon.

"Whatever it is, it's gonna break my line if I'm not careful."

Reggie picks up his fishing net and kneels down at the edge of the slope.

"Get it close to the surface, and I'll try to get the net on it, whatever it is."

Reggie reaches with the three-foot-long handle and dips the teardrop-shaped loop down into the water. He feels something large—maybe a log—and gets the net over it. He heaves and is surprised by the weight. He can't believe Pat's line hasn't broken already.

"What is it?" Pat asks.

"Can't see it." Reggie groans with the effort of trying to pull the thing up without falling into the water.

What soon surfaces from the water, Reggie's fishing net all tangled around it, is a human head, with the rest of the body visible just below the surface of the water. The face belongs to a man, its skin ghoulishly pale, its eyes sunken and milky inside cavernous sockets. A tongue pokes from the mouth like a swollen purple leech.

"Holy shit!" Reggie shouts, letting go of the net's aluminum handle as if it has suddenly become scalding hot.

Pat jerks his pole in terror and the line finally snaps. The body bobs at the surface for a moment before it begins to sink again. Before it disappears back into the murk, pulling the fishing net down with it, they can see that a heavy chain, like a vehicle tow cable, is wrapped around its shoulders and torso.

Reggie and Pat stare at the surface of the water, their chests heaving.

"Did I just see what I thought I saw?" Pat says.

"I'm afraid so," Reggie says.

"What do we do?"

"What do you think? We get the hell out of here and go call the police."

Oakland, California
September 19, 1980

KATE WRIGHT IS HOLDING her son, six-week-old Jeremy, at the kitchen table when her husband, Eric, comes into the room for breakfast. The baby boy fell asleep while nursing, and as Kate rises to put him in his crib, Eric kisses her on the forehead, careful not to jar the baby awake. He stands there for a moment, looking at his son cradled in his wife's arms.

"What an angel," he whispers, smiling.

Kate loves Eric's smile—it lights up his whole face with an expression of pure joy. That's one reason she fell in love with him—he's always happy, always smiling.

As Kate settles the baby into his crib in the bedroom, Eric pours himself a bowl of Kellogg's Frosted Mini-Wheats. Kate's tired from being up with the baby, but she comes back out to sit with Eric while he eats; she wants to spend a few minutes with her husband before he heads out for the day.

"I'm so glad you don't work for the sheriff's office anymore," she says.

"Me, too," Eric agrees.

"I worried all day long," Kate says. "I kept thinking something bad was going to happen."

"Nothing bad was going to happen to me," Eric says, taking a bite of his cereal.

Eric resigned from the sheriff's office last year. At thirty-one years old, he'd been a lieutenant—the youngest person ever to achieve that rank in Alameda County—but he'd claimed the job had become "too boring."

Although that's his usual excuse, Kate suspects he really quit to assuage her fears. Plus, they had the baby on the way—and Eric already has two older children from a previous marriage to help support—so she figures he wanted to find a more lucrative career anyway. Maybe he called police work boring to protect his reputation, or his own ego, but whatever the reason, she's genuinely thankful that he changed careers.

After he resigned from the sheriff's department, Eric took a job in a precious metals firm. He surprised Kate with his enthusiasm for the job, learning everything he could about the gold and silver business. She wouldn't have thought a man like her husband, always craving adventure, would have found learning about metals more exciting than police work, but Eric genuinely seemed to think so. As far as she could tell, he loved his new job and didn't have any regrets about giving up law enforcement.

Personally, she can certainly breathe easier now that he has a more ordinary nine-to-five job.

"Gotta go," Eric says, rising to put his empty bowl in the sink.

Kate walks him to the door and kisses him at the doorstep. The mid-September air outside is cool and pleasant.

"Are you working late again?" she asks.

"Nope," he says. "I'll be home in time for dinner."

He climbs into his Honda Civic and pulls out of the driveway. He sticks his arm out the window to wave at her, and she blows him a kiss good-bye.

She heads back to their bedroom and lies down, hoping to get a little more rest while the baby is asleep. As she drifts off, she thinks about how she'd never be able to relax this way if Eric was still working as a cop—she'd be anxious all day.

When the phone jars her awake a while later, it wakes the baby, too. She lifts the crying infant into her arms.

"Shhh. Shhh," Kate says, rocking Jeremy in her arms. Then she plucks the phone out of its cradle and tucks it into the crook of her neck. "Wright residence," she says, finally getting the baby calmed down.

"Hi, Kate. It's Dale over at the office. Is Eric there?"

Why would Eric's boss be calling? thinks Kate, her mind still foggy from sleep.

"No, he's on his way to work. He'll be there any..." She trails off because her eyes have found the clock hanging on the wall.

It's almost noon.

"Wait," she says, shaking her head to try to clear it. "Is Eric not at work this morning?"

"No," Dale says. "I figured he came down with something. But I need some information about one of our accounts."

Kate stares at the clock, now fully awake.

"Um, Dale," she says. "Eric left for work four hours ago. Are you sure he's not there?"

"Huh," Dale says. "That's strange. I hope nothing bad has happened."

THREE

KATE WRIGHT PACES the house for twenty minutes. She's afraid if she calls the police, they'll tell her it's too soon to open a missing person investigation. But she has another idea. She'll call her father, an Alameda County Municipal Court judge.

Her fingers tremble as they work the rotary dial.

"Dad," she says, "Eric's disappeared. I'm worried."

She explains the situation and is prepared for him to tell her not to be concerned about it. To her relief, he takes her worries seriously.

"I'll call the sheriff," he says. "I'll get them looking for him."

Her father tells her to try not to worry.

"He probably just had a flat tire or something," her father says.

Kate spends the day trying not to fall apart every time the baby cries. She calls a couple of friends and asks them to come over and sit with her, but they can't. One woman has to go into San Francisco for an appointment. The other has friends visiting and they're going to Alcatraz.

For much of the day, she sits on the front porch. She keeps the door open so she can listen for the baby and for the telephone. But she keeps an eye out, hoping that Eric's Honda Civic will pull up to the curb and he'll step out with an embarrassed smile on his face. He'll apologize for worrying her and have an excuse for why he was missing all day.

Every time a car approaches, she feels her heart swell with hope and then deflate from disappointment when it's not a Civic but a Ford pickup or a Chevy Nova or a Volkswagen Beetle. Occasionally a car that looks like his will approach, and the anticlimax is even more crushing.

His car never comes. Nor does the phone ring.

Finally, at close to five o'clock, her father's Mercury Grand Marquis pulls up in front of the house. Her dad steps out, still wearing his shirt and tie, his sleeves rolled to the elbow. Her father has always had a good poker face—as a judge, he's well practiced at hiding his emotions. But in her gut, Kate knows he's here to deliver bad news.

If it was good news, he would have called.

"Kate," he says, "let's go in the house."

"What happened?" she says, already feeling her knees go weak.

"I'll tell you inside," he says. "Where's the baby? Is Jeremy okay?"

"He's sleeping," she says, nearly shouting. "Tell me what happened."

"They found Eric's car."

"His car? Not him?"

"It was at the BART station at El Cerrito Plaza," he says. "I don't know how to say this, so I'm just going to give it to you straight. There was a bullet hole in the driver's side door and blood on the front seat."

From inside, as if he heard his grandfather's news, six-week-old Jeremy begins to wail.

WHILE KATE COULDN'T get anyone to come over on the day Eric disappeared, now she can't get people to leave her alone. For the next two days, a steady rotation of friends and family stop by to check in, keep her company, and help with the baby.

Everyone keeps telling her that Eric could be okay. To keep her spirits up. To try not to worry until they know more. But Kate knows her husband is dead. Everyone else is just fooling themselves.

Her father, who took the day off, is at the house when the sheriff's vehicle pulls up. A fresh-faced deputy steps out along with a veteran detective named Billy Horvath whom Kate recognizes from when Eric worked on the force.

"Ma'am," says the detective, "may we speak to you? Judge, you're welcome to join us."

"Have you found him?" Kate says.

"No," Horvath says, "but we do have some news."

When her father showed up with his news, she insisted on hearing it right away. But this time, Kate feels certain she knows what's coming, and she doesn't mind putting it off for a moment. She invites the men in and offers them coffee. They decline, and when Kate is finally seated across the table from them—with the baby sleeping soundly in the nursery—the detective gives her the update.

"The blood in Eric's car wasn't his," Horvath tells them. "It was animal blood."

"What?" Kate says, trying to make sense of what he's just told her.

"The crime lab confirmed the blood belonged to an animal," he says.

Before Kate has a chance to process this news, Horvath adds that the police searched Eric's office at work and found a book called *The Paper Trip*.

"Jesus Christ," her father says, smacking the table and shaking his head in disbelief.

But Kate feels lost. What's significant about the book?

"*The Paper Trip,*" Horvath explains, "is a notorious book about how to change your identity. It gives step-by-step instructions on what to do if someone wants to start a new life. How to obtain a new driver's license, Social Security card, birth certificate."

Kate stares at the detective, her emotions warring inside her. At first, she's relieved to think Eric might still be alive. But that relief quickly turns sour and bubbles into anger.

Did he abandon me and his infant son?

What kind of person would do that?

Kate expects her father to argue with the detective—to defend his son-in-law—but he says nothing to object.

"Ma'am," Horvath says to Kate, "we'd like your permission to search your residence. We want to see if we can find any additional evidence that supports our theory."

"Your theory?" Kate says, still confused and seeking clarification.

Horvath clears his throat, as if he didn't want to come right out and say what he's about to.

"Ma'am, we believe your husband faked his own death so he could run away and start a new life somewhere else."

PART 1

CHAPTER 1

Englewood, Colorado
October 1980

THIRTY-YEAR-OLD KATHI SPIARS speeds to work through the streets of Englewood, Colorado, just a few miles south of Denver. She expects this to be one of the last warm days of fall, and she has the top down on her Chevy Impala convertible. The wind whips her blond hair around her. The song "Renegade" by Styx is blasting on the radio. She taps her fingers on the steering wheel and sings along. To the west, the Rocky Mountains are visible, the peaks white with snow.

What a great day to be alive! she thinks.

Too bad she has to go to work.

She skids into the parking lot of a bar and restaurant called Mr. Greenjeans. Before she can turn the key to shut it off, the engine coughs and the car shudders. The engine backfires loudly—like a rifle shot—and the vehicle dies.

The damn thing runs like a charm...when it's actually running. But starting and stopping it is a challenge, and every time she catches a red light, she worries that the engine will fail on her. She hopes she can make enough in tips tonight to pay for a trip to the mechanic next week.

Kathi steps quickly through the parking lot; she's wearing high heels, a short denim skirt, and a black short-sleeved sweater. She prays that her manager, Frank—a gruff, no-nonsense Italian guy who looks a lot like the character Clemenza from *The Godfather*—won't give her a hard time about being late.

As she pushes through the front door, she's relieved to see that Frank is distracted. He's sitting at a table with a guy she doesn't recognize. One glance and she can tell what's happening: Frank is interviewing the stranger for a job.

She makes eye contact with the man, and he flashes her a big, almost goofy smile. Kathi can't help herself—the corners of her mouth curl up and she returns his smile with just a hint of her own. His eyes follow her as she walks behind the bar to punch her time card.

"You listening to me?" Frank says to the guy.

"Yeah, sorry," he says. "Got distracted."

"Well, try not to get distracted when you're on the clock. You're going to be working with her."

Fifteen minutes later, when Frank is holding the staff meeting to go over the table rotation and the night's specials, he introduces the stranger.

"What's your name again?" Frank asks.

"Steve," the guy says, looking right at Kathi as if the two of them are the only ones in the room. "Steve Marcum."

"Steve's going to be busing tables and doing other stuff to help out," Frank says. "Running meals. Cleaning up. If somebody clogs the toilet, let Steve here know and he'll plunge it."

This gets a laugh from everyone. Throughout his introduction, Steve keeps smiling. He has an expression on his face that's so wide-eyed, it's almost off-putting. Kathi doesn't know what to make of him. *The guy's gotta be thirty-some years old, and here he is about to start a job as a busboy—yet he's got a look on his face like he's on some great adventure. What gives?*

After the meeting breaks up, Steve approaches her and asks her name.

When she tells him it's Kathi, his smile broadens as if he's just gotten a great piece of news.

"Beautiful name," he says, clapping his hands together and laughing. "Kathi with a *K*?"

"Yes, with a *K*," she says, turning away.

"I've got a good feeling about you, Kathi with a *K*," Steve calls after her. "I think we're going to be great friends."

What a weirdo, she thinks as she walks away.

CHAPTER 2

THROUGHOUT THE DINNER RUSH, Kathi keeps seeing Steve. It's as if he always senses when she needs help. He's there to clear her tables, fill her customers' water glasses, empty their ashtrays. It's a busy night, but she has to admit he's helped make her life easier. She's sure he helps her more than he helps the other waitresses, and she finds herself flattered by the attention. He's starting to grow on her.

He's not bad-looking. At first, she hadn't given his appearance much thought. But the more she studies him, the more she realizes he's kind of cute. His hair is a dirty blond and his hairline is starting to recede. He has a square jaw and looks as though he could handle himself in a fight. But it's his perpetual grin—his constant good humor—that makes him attractive. He always has a look on his face that suggests he's in on some big private joke.

As the night goes on, the dinner crowd clears out, leaving customers lingering to drink cocktails and beers. After midnight, when business really starts to slow down, Frank invites the new guy to join him behind the bar in order to teach him how to mix drinks.

"You don't want to be a busboy forever, do you?" Frank says.

When Kathi approaches the bar and relays an order for drinks, Steve takes it as an opportunity to flirt with her.

"What are you doing here?" he asks.

"Getting drinks," she says, stating the obvious.

"No," he says. "I mean what are you doing *here*? In this bar. You should be on TV."

Kathi rolls her eyes, but secretly she's pleased.

"You should be on *Charlie's Angels*."

Kathi makes a *pfft* sound with her lips.

"I'm serious," Steve says, setting the drinks on her tray. "You're as pretty as Cheryl Ladd. Prettier."

"Do these lines normally work for you?" Kathi asks, turning to leave.

"I've never used them," Steve says. "I've never seen a woman like you before."

Kathi struts away, keeping her back to him. She doesn't want him to see how much she's smiling.

She can't help herself.

CHAPTER 3

AT THE END of the night, Kathi heads out to the parking lot. The cool air feels good on her skin after being cooped up in the stuffy, smoke-filled bar all night long. She decides to drive home with the top down.

Inside the car, she takes off her shoes—her toes are killing her—and presses the clutch with her bare foot.

Of course, the car won't start.

The engine sputters and stalls. The clutch whines loudly as she tries again.

"Can I help?"

She lifts her head and sees it's the new guy, Steve, approaching her car. He's wearing the same shit-eating grin he's had on his face all night. But as soon as he arrives at her door, the engine roars to life.

"Got it," she says, and can't help but return his smile with a smug one of her own.

She feels a small swelling of pride. *See?* she thinks. *I can take care of myself—I don't need a man to come to my rescue.*

"Have a good night," she says, shifting the car into reverse and preparing to take off.

"Say," he says, looking around as though he has just woken up and doesn't know how he got here, "do you know if the buses run this late?"

"You don't have a car?" Kathi asks, shifting back into neutral.

"Not at the moment," he says, again with that smile.

"Get in, Mr. *Charlie's Angels,*" she says. *Look who's rescuing who!*

They cruise up South Broadway toward Denver, the cool air pouring in around them. Steve tells Kathi that he only recently moved to Colorado.

"I love it here," he says. "It's so beautiful."

"Where are you from?" she asks.

"Oh, here and there. Everywhere."

"You move around a lot?"

"I've just been looking for the right place to settle down," he says. "I think Colorado's the place."

"Make it through the winter before you commit to that," she quips.

He tells her where he's staying, which turns out to be a motel over by the South Platte River. The place has seen better days. The color scheme was probably popular in the 1950s and hasn't been changed since. Beer bottles line the railing on the second floor, and it looks as though a few of them fell and shattered on the sidewalk below. Two letters are burned out on the VACANCY sign.

"This is just temporary," he says when they're in the parking lot, his grin faltering for the first time that night. "I'll be getting my own place soon."

He seems embarrassed for her to see the place where he's staying, and she wants to put him at ease.

"I get it," she says. "My place is no palace. I'm saving all the money I can. I've got plans."

"What are they?" he asks.

She's nervous the Impala's engine is going to die, so she shuts if off. They sit in the parking lot, talking. She tells him of her aspirations to open a hair salon in Glenwood Springs, Colorado.

"Have you ever been there?" she asks. "It's amazing. It has hot springs and skiing. Hiking and fishing."

"Sounds like you've got big plans," Steve says. "Any room for a man in those dreams with you?"

She gives him a sly smile. "Maybe."

His grin is gone, and now he stares at her, deadly serious.

"Would you like to go out with me sometime?" he says.

"Maybe," she says again, her tone sending a message that what she really means is *yes*.

CHAPTER 4

A MONTH LATER, Kathi wakes up in the morning next to Steve. There is enough sunlight slipping in through the blinds that she can see him clearly. She watches him as he sleeps, studying the calmness on his face. When he's awake, he's usually smiling or laughing—or at the very least has his eyes glued on her.

It's interesting to see him with a blank expression. He looks different. Tougher. Seeing him like this, she can imagine what he would look like if the smile ever goes away. She thought people were supposed to look more innocent when they slept, but he almost looks the opposite—he looks just a little bit mean.

A tiny bit sinister.

But if she's being honest with herself, she kind of likes that hint of roughness. Steve is a mysterious man, and she finds that mystery intriguing.

A lot has changed since they first met. Steve was quickly promoted from busboy to bartender. He bought a used pickup truck so he can drive back and forth to work. And he's also rented a small apartment, although he's been spending more time at her place than his.

He's wanted to explore Denver, get his bearings in the new city, and she's had a lot of fun being his tour guide. But what she'd really like is to learn more about him. She knows he's got a tragic past. A week ago over dinner, she finally got him to open up about his parents, both of whom died when he was in his midtwenties. When she asked if she could see a picture of them, he said his childhood home burned down when he was in high school—no one ever figured out the cause—and that's one reason he has so few possessions. His apartment contains no pictures of his parents, no family heirlooms, no items with any sentimentality attached to them at all.

"I don't get attached to things," Steve said, and then added pointedly, "I get attached to people."

Kathi was touched by the line at the time—she was smitten with him, too—but she still wants to learn more about him. To her, this is an important part of falling in love with someone—telling stories, sharing histories. Steve's been happy to get to know her. He asks her about her life all the time; it's when she turns the questions around on him that he becomes quiet or distracted.

She gets up to use the bathroom, and on her way past the window, she peeks out. Snow blankets the ground and more is falling from the sky in large flakes. As she slips back into bed, Steve begins to stir.

"Good morning, beautiful," he says, his signature smile spreading across his face.

"It's snowing," she says. "What do you say we spend the day in bed?"

"I like the sound of that," he says, and he moves his body toward hers.

"Not doing that." She laughs as he takes her into his arms. "Or not *just* that. I want to talk, too. I want to learn more about you."

Steve frowns and lets her go. He rolls onto his back.

"You never talk about yourself," Kathi says, leaning over him. She runs her fingernails through his chest hair. "I want to learn more about you."

"And then we can do the other thing?" he says, his ornery grin back.

"Yes," she says. "And then we can do the other thing."

He sits up in bed, leaning a pillow against the headboard for a backrest. He tilts his head, looking at the ceiling, apparently thinking hard about something.

Finally, he looks Kathi in the eye and says, "Look, Kathi, I'm really falling for you. So I'm just going to be honest with you. The whole truth. No secrets."

Kathi is touched. That's the kind of commitment she wants—no secrets.

"The truth is," Steve says, "I'm on the run."

"On the run?"

Kathi is shocked. What the hell is he talking about?

"I don't want anyone to find me."

Kathi feels sick with worry.

"Who are you running from?" she asks, not sure she wants to know the answer.

"My previous employer."

"And who's that?"

"The CIA," he says.

"The CIA? You mean the Central Intelligence Agency?"

"That's exactly what I mean," he says, and she can tell from the serious, unsmiling expression on his face that he's telling the truth. "I used to be a hit man for the government."

CHAPTER 5

ARE YOU KIDDING ME?" Kathi says, her mouth dropping open. "Is this some kind of joke?"

"I'm afraid not," Steve says in the most serious tone she has ever heard him use. "I used to kill people for a living."

Steve explains that he was drafted into the Marines and served as an infantry soldier during Vietnam. The government must have seen something in him, he tells Kathi, because when his tour was almost up, a guy in civilian clothes approached him on base and asked if he'd considered what he was going to do afterward.

"I told him I was going back home to California to find a job. He said, 'That would be a real waste for a man with your talent.' He handed me a business card with nothing on it but a first name and last initial. And a phone number."

Kathi doesn't know what to believe. Part of her wonders if Steve is full of crap. Another part of her thinks that she should dump him right away, quit her job, and do everything she can to make sure she never sees him again.

And yet another part—a part that she can hardly admit is there—is excited by the possibility that he's telling her the truth. Steve is a lot more interesting than the guys she's dated before. He has always seemed mysterious. He came to Colorado out of nowhere. He had hardly any possessions to his name, not even a car. Being an ex-CIA assassin actually makes a little bit of sense.

"I don't want to tell you the things I've done," he says to her now. "I'm putting you at risk enough as it is. But I want you to know two things. I never took a contract on a person who didn't absolutely deserve it. We're talking the worst kind of people on the planet. The world is a better place without them."

Kathi feels some measure of relief when he tells her this. At least he wasn't an assassin for the mob.

"Second," he says, "I'm done with that kind of work. I never want to go back to that world. I just want a normal, ordinary life."

Kathi stares at him. As preposterous as it sounds, everything he is saying makes sense. Steve always seems so damn happy—but now she gets why. He's been given a second lease on life. He's escaped the life he lived and now he's been given a do-over.

No wonder he always has a shit-eating grin on his face.

"I don't know what to say," she tells him. "I'm speechless. You swear you're telling the truth?"

"I swear on my mother's grave," he says, looking into her eyes with a puppy-dog expression. "I understand if you don't want to have anything to do with me. But if you break up with me, I'm going to have to ask you to keep this information quiet. I could be in real danger if it gets out."

Kathi stares at him, still trying to determine if this is all some kind of practical joke.

"I just want an ordinary life," he says. "And I really like you. I want you to be a part of that ordinary life."

Life with you, Kathi thinks, *doesn't sound like anything close to ordinary*.

Kathi smiles at him and shifts her position in bed so that she's sitting right next to him, her face inches from his.

"I'm not going to break up with you," she says, leaning in to give him a kiss. "Thank you for telling me the truth."

She wraps her arms around him in a tight embrace.

"Now that I've shared," Steve says, the corners of his mouth curving into his usual ornery grin, "can we make love now?"

She answers with a kiss.

IT'S NEW YEAR'S EVE, and Mr. Greenjeans is packed as the clock ticks toward midnight and the start of 1981. AC/DC plays over the speaker system, and all the customers have to shout to be heard. Steve is busy at the bar, passing beers and mixed drinks to the patrons. Kathi is running all over the room, trying to keep up. They are understaffed for such a busy night because so many employees wanted the night off to celebrate. But Kathi and Steve are making money hand over fist from all the tips.

They don't mind being here. They get to see each other.

As Kathi winds through the crowd toward the bar, one of the customers—a handsome guy who's been flirting with her all night—stops her and says, "How much for a kiss at midnight?"

"Sorry," she says, nodding her head toward Steve at the bar. "I'm already booked."

"That guy?" the customer says. "Oh, baby, you can do better than him."

She ignores the comment and glances at the bottle

of Coors in the guy's hand. It's only half empty but she asks if he wants another.

"If it means I get to see you back here in a minute, then absolutely."

At the bar, she puts in her drink orders for Steve to fill.

"Some guy just asked me for a kiss at midnight," she tells him, "but I said I already had plans to kiss someone."

She tells him this because she thinks he'll be flattered. And, maybe, she wants him to know that other men find her attractive—let him know how lucky he is to be with her.

But his expression turns tense and he wants to know which guy.

"It doesn't matter," she says, not wanting any trouble.

He puts the bottle of Coors on her tray along with other drinks for different customers. She heads back into the crowd.

When she hands the guy his Coors, he says, "Thanks, doll," and puts an arm around her waist. Her impulse is to pull away, but she doesn't want to seem rude—men who flirt often give the biggest tips.

"If you ever decide to leave your bartender and get with a real man," he says, moving his hand down to squeeze her butt, "let me know."

She pushes his hand away forcefully, glancing at Steve. She's horrified to see that he's staring at them. He almost looks as though he's going to come barreling through the crowd, ready to fight the guy, so she heads toward the bar to intercept him.

But instead of storming out from behind the bar, fists raised, Steve turns away and heads into the back room. Now Kathi feels even more mortified. Does he think she *wanted* that jerk to grab her ass?

She follows him into the back room, but there's no sign of Steve among the kegs and boxes of liquor. She spots the exit door ajar and peeks outside.

Steve is pacing in the falling snow, obviously angry.

"Are you okay?" Kathi says.

"I'm sorry," he says, clearly flustered.

"For what?" she says.

"For not killing that motherfucker who touched you!" he barks, pointing at the side of the building as if he can see the guy inside.

Kathi flinches. Steve goes back to pacing, his breath coming out in visible frosty bursts.

"It's okay," she says, although secretly, she *was* a little hurt when Steve ran off instead of defending her honor.

"You see, Kathi," he says, approaching her and putting his hands on her shoulders. Snowflakes stick to his hair. "There's something else I haven't told you."

"Tell me later," she says. "We need to get back. It's freezing out here."

"No," he says. "If I don't tell you now, I'm not sure I'll have the courage to go through with it later."

She feels antsy about getting back inside. Frank isn't going to be happy if he discovers that the two of them are outside chatting on the busiest night of the year.

Screw it, she tells herself. *Steve needs me right now. I'm going to listen.*

"I killed someone," Steve says.

"I know," Kathi says. "You were a hit man."

"No, I mean I killed someone else. I went to prison for it."

"Prison?" she says, as shocked as she was the day he first told her about the CIA.

"It was in a bar," he says, going back to pacing. "I was defending a woman who was being harassed by some jerk like that guy in there. He took a swing at me, and my training just took over. It was automatic. I broke the guy's neck. Just snapped it."

Kathi puts a hand over her mouth. She knows Steve killed people, but he'd never described what it was like before.

"I went to prison for manslaughter," he says. "That's another reason I'm on the run. The CIA was pissed at me. I think they were worried that I would say something. And killing a civilian is a big no-no. So when I got out, I decided to go into hiding."

He stares at her, his eyes watery from the cold. Kathi begins shivering, and she tells herself that it's from the cold, not from fear of Steve.

"When I saw that guy touch you," he says, "I wanted to go out there and say something. But I had to stop myself. I'm afraid of what I might do to him."

Kathi feels guilty for wishing Steve had come to her rescue. She doesn't want to put him in that position. Besides, she's a big girl—she can take care of herself.

"If it happens again, I'll go to prison till I'm a hundred," he says. "Or the CIA might make sure I never see my next birthday."

Inside, the crowd starts to count down toward midnight—their voices loud and drunk.

"I'm sorry I didn't come to your defense," Steve says, his voice trembling.

She wraps her arms around him. "You did the right thing," she says. "I don't want you to kill anyone. I don't want you to go to prison. I want you here with me."

The crowd cheers as the clock strikes midnight. Out in the alley behind the bar, Steve holds Kathi in his arms and kisses her. They press their bodies together. As they kiss, Kathi realizes she's never loved anyone the way she loves Steve Marcum.

He's her best friend.

Her lover.

Her soul mate.

And in this moment, kissing him in the first seconds of 1981, she feels certain that it's just a matter of time before he's her husband.

CHAPTER 7

Spring 1981

KATHI IS RIDING the bus home from her afternoon shift. The bus is crowded and the air inside is hot, with a slight odor. It's like being in a men's locker room on wheels. She's taking public transportation because her Impala finally crapped out. She didn't really understand all the technical jargon that the mechanic was using, but Steve translated it for her: "The car is toast," he said, smiling as he always did.

She has enough money saved up to either repair it or buy another used car, but she can't bring herself to dip into her savings for either. She and Steve plan to quit their jobs this summer and head somewhere new. They've been getting by on sharing his pickup, but he took the day off today and said he needed the truck. So she's stuck on the cramped bus, trying not to get sick breathing in the clammy air.

Lately, Steve has been paying for everything. Dinners. Dates. He even covered her rent last month, saying that since he was at her place more than his, he might as well help out. She doesn't know where the money's coming from. He doesn't make any more than she does. But whenever she asks him about it, he always tells her that he has a little money from his father's estate.

"How much?" she'll ask.

"Enough," he'll say.

When she gets off the bus a few blocks from her apartment, the air outside feels refreshing. It's been a warm day, but evening is approaching and the temperature is already dropping.

She looks ahead to see if Steve's pickup is parked in the street. It's not there. In its usual place sits a red Porsche adorned with ribbons like a birthday gift.

Wow, I wonder who that's for, Kathi thinks.

As she gets closer, Steve comes out of her apartment building and into the street, the biggest grin she's ever seen on his face. He gestures toward the Porsche.

"What do you think?" he says. "Do you like it?"

Kathi's mouth drops open. "Is that yours?" she asks.

"No, silly. It's yours."

Kathi gasps. She circles the car, her mouth still agape. It's a beautiful machine. The sunlight glints off the perfectly polished paint.

"Steve, is this some kind of joke?"

"No," he says, "and neither is this."

With that, he drops to one knee in the middle of the street and reaches into his back pocket. Kathi stares, stunned, as he opens a small box to reveal a diamond engagement ring. The diamond looks big enough to make her wonder which cost more: the car or the ring.

"Kathi Spiars," Steve says, "I've never met anyone like you. I want to spend the rest of my life with you. Will you marry me?"

Kathi can't believe what's happening. Not so much the proposal—she'd felt Steve would propose sooner or later. But the extravagance of the purchases has her taken aback. *How can Steve afford this?*

She pushes those thoughts out of her mind. He was trying to surprise her, and he's certainly done it.

"Steven Marcum," she says, "I've certainly never met anyone like *you*. Yes, I'll marry you."

Steve lifts her into the air, and the two kiss.

Kathi vows to talk to Steve about all this spending. In her mind, they're saving toward a life together. She needs to get a sense of just how much money he has—and where it all came from—and she wants them to both be on the same page in terms of how it should be spent. They shouldn't squander their money on high-price luxuries they don't need.

But for right now, she's going to enjoy her moment with him—and enjoy the extravagance of it.

"How should we celebrate?" Steve asks when they finally stop kissing.

"I've got an idea," she says.

"What?"

"Let's take the car for a spin!"

CHAPTER 8

"THIS PLACE IS DEAD TONIGHT," Steve says to Kathi over the telephone. "I'm bored to death."

"It's only a couple more weeks," she says into the receiver.

She stands in the apartment kitchen, where the phone is mounted to the wall. The room is cool, and she's ready to climb back under the covers. She was reading a book in bed when he called.

They live together now, and most of their shifts are together, but tonight is a rare night when Steve is working without Kathi. The wedding date is set, and they've both given their notice to Frank that they're leaving. But ever since they gave notice, Steve has been talking about ditching his final shifts. At first Kathi ignored it, but the more he complains, the more she realizes he's serious. It surprises her a little—she's never once considered cutting out early. She promised to finish her two weeks while Frank looked for a replacement, and she doesn't want to break her word.

"Just hang in there," she tells him, twisting the

phone cord out of habit. “It’s not as if you’re being tortured.”

“Boredom *is* torture,” Steve moans dramatically. “Not being with you *is* torture.”

Kathi laughs and tells him she loves him. After she returns the phone to its cradle, she climbs back into bed and picks up the Robert Ludlum novel she checked out of the library. Ever since Steve told her that he was in the CIA, she’s been interested in reading stories of espionage. She’s sure that Steve’s experiences were nothing like the fictional adventures of Jason Bourne. But Steve won’t—or can’t—talk about the things he did, so she’s been drawn to these types of fantasies instead.

About an hour later, Kathi finds herself distracted by a noise down the hall. The toilet is running. She can hear water filling the tank. She gets out of bed, dropping the book on the bedspread, and heads to the bathroom. She jiggles the toilet’s handle and waits a few moments, hoping it will stop.

It doesn’t.

“Ugh,” she grunts, grabbing the lid to the toilet tank and hefting it off.

She sets it on the floor as gently as she can and stands back up to peer into the tank. She gasps. Down in the bottom of the tank, submerged in water, are two stacks of what look like gold bars.

“What on earth?” Kathi says aloud.

She reaches into the cold water and lifts one of the metal bars. It’s not much bigger than a candy bar, but she can’t believe how heavy it is. She vaguely remembers reading somewhere that although gold is soft and malleable, it is also very dense.

Very heavy.

She examines the bar, finding no markings or

engravings. But it *must* be gold—real gold; she's sure of it. She can't imagine it could be anything else. She looks into the tank and counts the bars. There are six in total, including the one in her hand.

Wasn't there something on the news the other night about how the value of gold is through the roof right now—an all-time high? Now that she's thinking about it, Steve *had* paid close attention during that part of the program. Kathi hadn't been particularly interested. Who cares about gold? She couldn't afford any. But Steve had risen from his seat and turned up the volume.

Heart racing, Kathi sets the gold bar back in the water and then lifts the lid and covers the tank. She dries off her arm and begins pacing through the house.

What the hell is going on?

Who the hell am I about to marry?

Steve confessed about being in the CIA. He admitted to killing someone in a bar fight and spending time in prison. But he never said anything about a stash of gold bars.

Somehow, this discovery has her rattled. Even though he told her about the CIA and prison, some part of her hasn't fully believed him. This is the first tangible evidence of Steve's secret life, something physical that he's brought from that old life into this new one. At least she hopes it was from his past, not some new escapade he's keeping a secret from her.

As she paces through her bedroom, she stops and stares at the spy novel she's been reading.

Maybe Steve Marcum's adventures were *as exciting as Jason Bourne's,* she thinks.

Just then, she hears keys at the front door.

Steve strolls into the apartment with a big smile on his face. Kathi knows why: he's closed early and ditched work. He has a pleased-with-himself, I-do-what-I-want look about him.

But one glance at her face tells him that something is amiss. His grin vanishes.

"What's wrong, baby?" he says. "You're not mad that I left early, are you?"

Kathi doesn't know what to say. Should she tell him she found his stash?

She doesn't want any secrets between them. If she doesn't ask now, when will she ask? On the eve of their wedding?

"When were you going to tell me?" she asks.

"About what?"

"What do you think?" Kathi says. "Are you keeping other secrets from me besides the gold bricks in the toilet?"

CHAPTER 9

STEVE STARES AT HER, and for just a moment—a time so brief that she'll later tell herself her mind was playing tricks on her—he looks truly sinister. Kathi knows he's a man who is (or at least was) capable of killing people.

Then the corners of his mouth turn up and he bursts out laughing, a big boisterous chuckle that raises the tension in the room rather than dispelling it.

"That's some pretty good sleuthing," he says. "You would have made a decent CIA operative yourself." Then, under his breath but loud enough for her to hear, he mutters, "I knew I should have fixed that damn toilet."

"I'm serious, Steve. That *is* gold, isn't it?"

He nods and takes her hand. "Of course," he says. "It's the real thing. It's from my parents' estate. My inheritance."

"What the hell is it doing in the toilet?"

"It's the safest place in the apartment," he says, shrugging as if the answer is obvious. "If the building burns down, the toilet will still be there, keeping the gold nice and cool. I'll know right where it is."

Kathi stares at him, dumbfounded.

"How do you think I bought your Porsche?" he says, and then gestures to the ring on her finger. "And that?"

He has such a happy look on his face that she wants to burst out laughing. One of the things she loves most about being with Steve is how he acts as though the world is a big joke—and he wants her to be in on the joke with him.

But she can't laugh off the absurdity this time.

She needs some goddamn answers.

"I don't know if I can do this, Steve."

"Do what?"

"This," she says, practically shouting. She holds her hands up to suggest that she's talking about everything in the apartment—their whole life together. "I don't know if I can live with all the secrets. I love you, Steve, but I'm not sure who *you* are."

Steve says he's sorry he didn't tell her about the gold. He wanted her to love him for who he is, not for his money. He doesn't like to touch the money—the car and the ring were rare extravagances for him—and he'd rather use it every now and then, on an as-needed basis.

"It's an investment in my future," he says. "*Our* future. I think of it like a retirement fund or a CD. As long as the price of gold continues to rise, I don't want to sell it."

Kathi wants to ask how much it's worth, but she's afraid that will give him the wrong impression.

"I don't need your money," she says. "I don't love you because you're rich."

"I know," he says. "But that's why I didn't tell you. I've been honest about everything else."

Kathi argues that while Steve has told her some information about his past, he's been vague about the details. He's still secretive. He's still a mystery to her.

"What do you want to know?" he says, his mood darkening. "You want to know what a man looks like when your fingers are wrapped around his throat? You want to know about the moment when you choke the life out of him? It's not like in the movies, Kathi. You can tell by looking in the eyes when the lights go out inside. One minute the person looking back at you is alive. The next?" He snaps his fingers. "Gone. Dead. You can see it, Kathi—you can see it in the eyes: the moment when life turns to death. Is that the kind of thing you want me to talk about?"

"Jesus Christ—*no!*" Kathi snaps, her body covered in goose bumps.

"Because that's who I am," Steve says. "That's who I was before I met you. And if you don't want to be with me, tell me now. I'll walk out that door and you'll never see me again."

Tears fill Kathi's eyes.

"That's not what I want," she says, trying to keep from sobbing. "And that's not who you are. Not now. And I don't believe that's all there is to your past. I just want to know more about you. Where you went to high school. Where you grew up."

"I told you, my house burned down." Steve says the words defensively, but his tone has softened.

"Then show me where it used to be," Kathi says. "Show me the neighborhood. Show me something. I don't even know where you grew up. What city? What state?"

Steve takes a deep breath.

"You want me to show you where I'm from?"

"Yes," Kathi says. "Please."

"All right," Steve says, pointing to the door. "Let's go."

"What? Now?"

"Pack an overnight bag. Let's leave in fifteen minutes."

Kathi doesn't quite know what to make of this.

"I'm wide awake," he says. "I'll drive all night."

"Where are we going?"

"California."

CHAPTER 10

ABOUT FORTY-FIVE HOURS LATER, Steve is at the wheel of Kathi's Porsche, cruising through the Mojave Desert at seventy miles an hour. The sun is setting to the west, and the orange light gives the desert hills a strange otherworldly glow.

Steve has his sun visor pulled down and is squinting against the bright orange light they're driving directly toward. When the sun finally disappears, Steve takes a deep breath and says, "Finally." He flips the visor up and rubs his eyes.

Kathi feels tempted to say that if they'd gotten a move on earlier this morning, they wouldn't have had to drive directly into the sunset. But she bites her tongue. The farther they've driven into California, the worse Steve's mood has gotten.

When they left home in the middle of the night, Steve was enthusiastic and Kathi was excited for the adventure. Steve drove through the night, just as he said he would, but by the time they made it to Las Vegas late the next morning, he wanted a break.

"I need a nap," he said.

"I can drive," Kathi offered, since she'd slept for a couple of hours during the night.

"We still have a long way to go," he said. "Let's both get some rest."

Instead of resting, though, Steve had gone to play blackjack on the Strip. Kathi spent the afternoon at the pool where they were staying, though she'd had to buy a bathing suit at the hotel gift shop. She hadn't known she'd need one.

Steve returned to the hotel room drunk that evening as she was getting ready for bed. He said they should go elope right there in Las Vegas. He was acting as though he'd forgotten the whole point of their trip, as if maybe this was a vacation in Nevada and nothing more. But Kathi wouldn't let him forget. And even though she wanted to marry him, the timing didn't feel right. She'd given him an ultimatum to show her something of his past, and she intended to stick to it.

The next morning, she was ready and raring to go. She bought breakfast and brought it back to the room, hoping for an early start. But Steve said they should enjoy Vegas a little more and insisted they sit by the pool while he slurped cocktails. It was well into the afternoon when Kathi finally put her foot down and said they needed to leave before he had another drink.

He's been sulking ever since.

But Kathi doesn't care. If he wants her to marry him, he is going to have to share more about himself. This is his opportunity.

They drive through Bakersfield without talking. The car is pointed north now, on a trajectory up through California's Central Valley.

Practically the middle of nowhere.

Kathi has no idea where they're going but knows they must be close because Steve's mood is darkening.

As he takes the exit to a town called Exeter, his fingers are wrapped so tightly around the steering wheel, it's as though he's trying to strangle it.

It occurs to Kathi that this trip might be very painful for him. His parents are both dead. His childhood home burned down. Who knows what else happened to him in this town? There is probably a good reason he never talks about where he came from.

"Are you okay?" she asks, trying to sound compassionate.

"I'm fine," he says in a tone that tells her he is anything but. "You wanted to see my past. I'll show you my past."

He drives through Exeter without saying a word. The streets are empty, the storefronts dark. There is a water tower, a grocery store, a small cinema with its marquee advertising a horror double feature: *The Howling* and *Friday the 13th Part 2*. The town can't have much more than five thousand residents. It looks like a lot of small towns in Colorado, only with fields of orange trees instead of hills of pine forest.

Kathi doesn't know where Steve is going, and it doesn't seem as though he does, either. He cruises around, staring out at the moonlit streets. Suddenly, as if a thought occurred to him, Steve yanks the wheel and turns a corner hard enough that the tires squeal. He zooms down a back road.

And stops at a cemetery.

"You want to know about my past?" he says sarcastically. "I'll take you to meet my parents."

CHAPTER 11

THE GATE IS OPEN and they drive in among the tombstones, which cast long shadows in the ghostly moonlight. An absurd thought pops into Kathi's head that if Steve wanted to kill her, this would be a perfect place to do it.

She shoves the thought away but still feels sick to her stomach. Steve is obviously angry with her. This isn't some pleasant trip down memory lane for him.

Without a word, he leaves the car and stomps into the graveyard. She follows but can't keep up. He clomps through the grass, ducking his head to try to read the names on the gravestones. There is enough moonlight that the words can be deciphered, but only with some effort.

"Goddamnit," he growls. "Where are they?"

Kathi starts looking, too, desperate to find the name Marcum so that she can relieve some of his anxiety. It's her fault they are here.

Steve keeps cursing, but his voice cracks and she can tell he is crying.

"Steve, honey, are you okay?"

"I can't find it," he sobs. "They took it."

He collapses to his knees and puts his face in the grass. His body convulses with sobs.

"They took everything!" he wails.

"Who?"

"The CIA," he says. "They've erased my existence."

Kathi isn't sure what he means—did the CIA remove his parents' grave markers?—but she can see he is suffering. Over the past few months, she's questioned some of the things Steve has told her. His stories about the CIA and prison seem a little far-fetched. But there is no questioning this: Whatever has come over him, her fiancé is in real pain.

Kathi puts her arms around Steve.

"It's okay," she says. "You're okay."

He hugs her, still crying. "I don't want to be here," he says. "It's too painful. I don't want to lose you, but it's too painful."

She's reminded that Steve came here *for* her. This place is clearly a source of trauma, and yet he's made the trip to appease her. It's almost as if he's walked through fire because she asked him. She can't help but feel touched by his attempt. She decides in this moment to give up asking Steve about his past. None of that matters.

She knows the real Steve Marcum in her arms.

"I love you," she whispers to soothe his pain. "Let's go home. Let's go make a life together."

Wiping tears from his face, he says, "You mean it?"

"I've never meant anything more."

CHAPTER 12

June 6, 1981

KATHI TAKES A DEEP BREATH.

Today is the day.

She and her bridesmaids stand inside a large tent on a warm summer day, waiting for Mendelssohn's "Wedding March" to begin. She feels anxious to get out of the tent. There is a pleasant breeze outside, and inside the tent, the air is stuffy.

She's hiding here because Steve hasn't seen her yet—it's bad luck to see the bride before the wedding, after all.

"You look beautiful," says Sarah, her maid of honor, a friend from high school she's stayed in touch with ever since.

Kathi is wearing a white gown with lace overlays covering her arms and a lace skirt that flares at her hips. Her hair is pulled up and a crown of flowers adorns her head. She holds a bouquet of pink peonies. "Thank you," she says. She'll be hearing that compliment a lot today.

"Are you ready for this?" Sarah asks.

"As ready as I'll ever be," Kathi says, and the two giggle.

The music begins, loud and dramatic, as if announcing the entrance of a queen. After the bridesmaids have left, Kathi waits for her cue and steps out into the sunlight. Fifty guests rise from their seats, turn, and look at her.

The breeze is immediately refreshing, and she takes a big, joyful breath before starting forward. Her hands tremble and she grips the flowers tightly to still them. She smiles at all the faces—family, friends, coworkers—and every one of them smiles back at her.

At the end of the aisle, standing next to the minister underneath the flower-covered wedding arch, Steve gives her his big signature grin. Their wedding is happening in a meadow filled with wildflowers, with the Rocky Mountains standing as the picturesque backdrop.

She couldn't have asked for a more perfect day.

When she arrives at the altar, Steve raises his eyebrows comically, as if to say, *We're really doing this, aren't we?*

Yes, we are, Kathi thinks, and there isn't a doubt in her mind that this is what she wants.

Steve is wearing an all-white tuxedo, matching her dress. The only color on it is the pink peony pinned to his breast pocket, matching her bouquet.

He's not traditionally handsome—it's not as if he turns the head of every woman who walks by—but *she* finds him attractive. He's combed over his sandy blond hair to cover where it's thinning. He can just let the hair go, as far as she's concerned. His smile and his eyes and the way he looks at the world are what caught her attention from the start, and she can't believe that she gets to join him on an adventure through life.

He's kind and treats her well, but he's also spontaneous—and to be honest, she knows his impulsiveness is what she really loves about him.

She knows that a life with Steve Marcum will not be boring.

The officiant begins going through his script, but Kathi is too consumed with love and happiness to even follow the words. She hardly pays attention until it's time for her to say her vows. Kathi blinks back tears of happiness as she stares up at Steve, who is crying and looking at her the way no man ever has.

"Please repeat after me," the minister says. "I, Kathi..."

She repeats what the minister says.

"...take thee, Steve, to be my wedded husband...to have and to hold, from this day forward, in sickness and in health..."

Kathi means it with all her heart when she says aloud for all her friends and family to hear, "Till death do us part."

PART 2

Glenwood Springs, Colorado
Spring 1993

IT'S BEEN SO GREAT CHATTING," says Sarah, "but I've got to run. These kids won't feed themselves."

Kathi laughs into the cordless telephone. She takes a sip of her tea and sets it on the coffee table. The night is cold—there's still some snow on the ground outside—but a fire burns in the fireplace. The TV is muted while an episode of *America's Funniest Home Videos* plays.

She and Steve share a ranch-style cabin, with an expansive living space and vaulted ceiling spanned by large oak beams. The rustic mountain decor includes old wooden skis and cane fishing poles as decorations, along with paintings of elk and bear. A deer mount hangs on one wall, the rifle that Steve used to shoot it displayed underneath.

"Let's not wait so long to catch up again," Kathi says.

She's spent the past hour talking to her old friend, who got married a year after Kathi and Steve and has lived in Denver, raising her family, ever since. They live only about two and a half hours away, but it's been years since Kathi has seen her friend. Sarah and her husband have two children—a ten-year-old girl and a six-year-old boy—and are living what Steve would probably call a "stupid boring suburban life."

Kathi and Steve have done the opposite. Over the past decade, they've moved all around Colorado, spent a year in Mexico, and even lived for a spell in Southern California while working at Disneyland. She expected life with Steve to be anything but normal, and her predictions proved accurate. But in the past few years, things have settled down a bit, and if she's honest, she prefers life this way.

The gold bars Steve used to keep in the toilet wherever they lived have long since disappeared; assuming Steve is telling the truth, he traded them in for a little extra money here and there as they've needed it.

They traded in the Porsche for more practical automobiles better suited to life in Colorado.

Now that they've settled here in Glenwood Springs, Kathi expects most of their transient adventuring days to be over. With its hot springs, ski resorts, and endless hiking trails, Glenwood Springs is everything Kathi needs right now, and she can see herself growing old here with the man she loves.

She owns a salon, just as she always dreamed, and they've bought a house. She's been the breadwinner for years now. It was her savings, not his, that allowed her to buy the salon. But Steve has a steady job managing one of the local steam baths the town is known for. Although he had no real qualifications for the job, when he left for his interview, he said, "Don't worry, Kathi, I could sell ice to Eskimos. This job is mine."

But Kathi won't be surprised if Steve comes home someday soon with another harebrained scheme to pick up and move on to the next adventure. Talking to Sarah, Kathi actually found herself feeling jealous of her friend's "stupid boring suburban life."

She's also feeling very nostalgic after reminiscing with Sarah about their high school days: funny things that happened in class, practical jokes they used to play, boys they used to date. After she hangs up with Sarah, she rises from the couch and heads into the spare bedroom, where she opens the closet and roots around among the boxes inside. At last, she pulls open a dusty cardboard box and finds exactly what she's searching for: her high school yearbook.

With a smile on her face, she heads back to the living room. After refilling her cup of tea and throwing another log on the fire, she sits on the couch and flips through the volume, laughing to herself as she sees the youthful faces of all her peers.

She stops at her own senior portrait and can't believe how young she looked. Has it really been twenty-five years since she graduated from high school? She feels a pang of sadness. Life feels as though it's slipping away, and what has she done with her time? Sure, she's had fun with Steve. But their life together also seems to lack the kind of security her friend Sarah has enjoyed. Kathi tells herself she's just feeling emotional from the phone call.

She hears the garage door rising and a minute later Steve walks in the door, pulling off his coat and tossing his keys on the counter.

"What's up?" he says.

"Just going down memory lane," she says.

He joins her on the couch and his eyes widen when he sees her high school picture.

"Wow," he says, giving her the bright smile she fell in love with all those years ago.

"I know," she says. "Look how pretty I used to be."

"You're as beautiful as ever," he says, kissing her cheek. "You haven't aged at all since I met you."

She makes a *pfft* sound with her lips, but she's touched.

And she could say the same about Steve. He's put on a few pounds and lost more of the hair on his scalp, but he still has the same boyish face he had twelve years ago. The same ornery-schoolboy smile.

Nothing ever seems to stress him out.

That must be his secret.

Kathi flips through the yearbook and shows him other pictures of herself: posing as a cheerleader, with friends by a line of lockers, standing with the student council. She tells him that she only became student council secretary because she had a crush on the class president.

"You know," Steve says, "I was student body president."

"You were?" Kathi says, surprised. "At Exeter?"

Steve shares so little about his past that she's delighted he has told her this.

"Is that so hard to believe?" he says.

"You?" she says. "I don't see it."

"If I'm lying, I'm dying," he says.

"I'm going to need some photographic proof," she jokes. "Where's your high school yearbook?"

Steve's smile falters.

"I don't have it," he says. "It burned up in the fire."

"Oh, damn," Kathi says, feeling terrible. "I'm so sorry. I didn't mean to..." She trails off, not sure how to finish.

If possible, she generally tries not to bring up topics like his dead parents, his burned childhood home, or the CIA—nothing from his past that might stir up bad memories.

Steve shrugs, unbothered.

"If you were student body president," she says, treading lightly, "you must have been very popular."

"I guess I had a lot of friends," he says. "I was voted Most Dependable."

"Most Dependable?" She laughs. "I didn't even know there was such a thing."

On the one hand, Kathi is not surprised to hear this—Steve seems like someone who would have had a lot of friends and could've been voted something like Most Dependable in the class superlatives. On the other hand, what *is* surprising is him actually talking about it.

After twelve years of marriage, is he finally going to open up?

"It's too bad my yearbook burned up with everything else," he says. "You could've seen what I looked like when I had hair."

"I can't imagine," she jokes, giggling.

Steve tells Kathi he's going to take a shower before dinner, and he leaves her alone in the living room with her yearbook. She flips through the pages, but her mind is on Steve and how he can't even enjoy the simple pleasure of looking at old photographs.

She has an idea. She can't do anything about the family pictures he lost in the fire when he was a kid, but she tells herself that she'll call his old high school tomorrow.

After all, their twelve-year wedding anniversary is coming up soon. They never spend much money on gifts for each other, opting instead for personal items that have significant meaning for the other person.

A copy of his old yearbook would make the perfect gift for Steve.

CHAPTER 14

EXETER UNION HIGH SCHOOL," says the voice on the other end of the line. "How may I help you?"

"Hi," Kathi says, trying to sound as friendly as possible. "This might sound like a strange request, but I'm trying to get hold of a yearbook for the class of 1967."

"A yearbook?" the woman says, sounding confused.

"My husband graduated in 1967, and I'm trying to find a copy of the yearbook. His burned up in a fire."

"Oh," the woman says. "Let me see if I can find someone to help you."

As she waits on hold, Kathi tucks the phone into the crook of her neck and busies herself with some accounting. She's sitting behind the front desk in her salon, which usually has a lull in business in the middle of the afternoon. One stylist is giving a woman a perm and another is doing a pedicure, but otherwise the place is empty. Kathi expects that school has probably just let out in California.

Outside her window, she watches residents walk up

and down the sidewalk along Main Street. It's a typical day in Glenwood Springs. The outdoor supply store is offering a big sale to get rid of its stock of winter clothing. The bookstore has a buy-two-get-one-free sale going on. The local theater marquee lists *Indecent Proposal* and *Sommersby* as the current features. She saw the latter with a girlfriend and thought it was entertaining enough, aside from its preposterous premise about a man assuming someone else's identity.

"Any day now?" Kathi mutters, checking the clock and mentally doing the math about how much this phone call has already cost her.

She wanted to make the call from her business phone in case Steve saw their phone bill and wondered why she'd made a long-distance call to his hometown. That would ruin the surprise of the anniversary present.

A male voice comes on the line: "Hello, this is Percy Hickman. I teach history here, and I'm the faculty adviser for the yearbook. I understand you're trying to purchase an old yearbook?"

Kathi explains what she is trying to do and why. She hopes there is a stockpile of extra copies of old yearbooks in a closet somewhere and that it won't be a problem to purchase one.

"Class of '67, you say?"

"Yes," Kathi confirms.

"What a coincidence," Percy exclaims. "I graduated in '67, too."

The man sounds very excited, and it takes Kathi a moment to understand what he's getting at.

"Wait," she says. "You graduated from Exeter in 1967? The same school *and* year as my husband?"

"Sure did," he says. "I never thought I'd come back and be a teacher in the school I graduated from, but here I am teaching in the same classroom where I used to stick bubble gum under the desks. Life is funny like that."

Kathi is excited about the idea of speaking to a classmate of Steve's. She's never met anyone who knew him before her. No friends. No family. No one.

"You must know my husband," she says. "Steve Marcum."

After a pause, Percy says, "Hmm. Sorry. It doesn't ring a bell."

Confused, Kathi says, "He was student body president."

"No," Percy says. "Not the class of '67. I should know. I was on the council, and we haven't heard from our president in a good fifteen years. I've been stuck organizing all the reunions."

Kathi wonders if maybe she's gotten the year wrong but feels certain that Steve's always said he graduated in '67, two years before her.

"Are you sure the name Steve Marcum doesn't sound familiar?" Kathi asks. "Friendly guy. Spontaneous. I bet he would have been a lot of fun in high school."

"Our graduating class wasn't that big," Percy says. "I thought I remembered everyone. But I've probably forgotten a name or two."

Kathi can't see how anyone could forget Steve. He has the kind of personality that makes him memorable. She doubts he was much different when he was in high school. And besides, if this guy is in charge of organizing the reunions, he should have a master list of every student.

Something doesn't add up here.

"You sure he lived in Exeter, California?" Percy asks. "Maybe he went to the one in New Hampshire. Or England."

Percy suggests she check with her husband and

make sure she's got the right class and the right school.

Kathi frowns at the man's unhelpful comments. Of course Steve grew up in Exeter, California. She'll never forget the drive they took there and the way he broke down at the cemetery.

Although…thinking back on it now, Kathi realizes that she never actually saw the gravestones. A worm of doubt crawls into her mind.

"Miss," Percy says, "you still there?"

"Anyway," Kathi says, "can you send me the year-book?"

The man protests, saying he's sure the book won't have what she's looking for. Kathi insists that she wants it regardless, and arranges to send a check to cover the price of the book and postage.

Before they end the call, Kathi asks Percy, "By the way, what was the name of your class president?"

"Eric Wright."

"Never heard of him," Kathi says.

CHAPTER 15

KATHI FORGETS ABOUT her conversation with Percy Hickman until a couple of weeks later, when she comes home and finds a book-size package in the mailbox. She looks around as if she's doing something clandestine. Steve isn't home yet, so she hurries into the house and tears into the package.

"I'll show you," she mutters, thinking of the smug history teacher who was so sure that Steve didn't graduate from Exeter in 1967.

She flips immediately to the senior class and scans through the names alphabetically. She finds no Steve Marcum.

"Damn," she mumbles, disappointed.

That means she was either mistaken or Steve lied to her. And to her knowledge, Steve hasn't lied to her since they got married. He admitted going to prison and killing people for the CIA, for Christ's sake. If that's not honesty, she doesn't know what is.

She turns to the table of contents and finds the page number for the photo of the school council. Her heart lifts when she sees Steve's familiar smiling face pictured with a group of teenagers. He's younger—and he has a full head of hair—but the smile on the kid is unmistakable. She stares, captivated, at the eighteen-year-old version of her husband. She's never seen a photo of him from before she met him, and it warms her heart to see him at that age.

They've had some ups and downs over the past decade, but at this moment, staring at the youthful Steve Marcum, she knows she loves him as much as she ever has.

Her eyes drop to the photo caption, and her heart sinks again. The name Steve Marcum does not appear in the caption. She looks back and forth between the picture and the caption to determine what name they've attributed to Steve.

The caption says the boy pictured is named Eric Wright.

She tells herself this is just some sort of mistake. And maybe if the only evidence was the yearbook, she would be able to convince herself of that. But there's also the teacher, Percy—he said their student body president was named Eric Wright. Why would that be the case if there was simply an editing error in the book?

No. There's something else going on here.

And the only conclusion she can draw is that her husband has been lying to her for the past twelve years.

She flips to the superlatives and scans through the pictures. Class Clown...Cutest Couple...Most Likely to Succeed. There it is: Most Dependable.

As before, a young version of her husband is pictured. And again as before, the name listed is Eric Wright.

She finds pictures of him with the tennis, wrestling, and baseball teams—all of them without a doubt her husband, all of them with the name Eric Wright. She turns back to the senior class, and this time turns to the names that begin with *W*. Sure enough, Eric Wright is listed.

Once again, Steve's smiling photo is next to the name.

But now Kathi interprets his signature smile differently. Now she sees something dark in his expression. There's always been some mischievousness in that smile, but now it seems almost malevolent. She once thought he smiled as if there was some kind of big joke going on that no one else saw. She always liked that about him. But looking at him as a boy, knowing the man who would grow up and lie to her, she doesn't feel smitten with that smile. She feels betrayed by it.

She always thought Steve wanted her to be in on the joke.

But maybe the joke is on her.

CHAPTER 16

THE NEXT DAY, KATHI again dials the number for Exeter Union High School. This time she specifically asks to speak with Percy Hickman. The salon is nearly empty, but still she keeps her voice down as if she's not supposed to be making this call. Outside her window, a cinema employee is taking down the SOMMERSBY letters and replacing them with CLIFFHANGER, the new Sylvester Stallone movie she's seen advertised on TV.

Last night she debated whether to confront Steve and decided she was too afraid. Something in her gut told her she needed more answers before she could talk to her husband.

"Hello, this is Percy Hickman."

"I'm the one who called about ordering the 1967 yearbook," Kathi says. "It just arrived yesterday."

Percy says he remembers her and asks if she was able to find what she was looking for.

"Not exactly," she says. "I was hoping you could tell me a little more about this Eric Wright."

"Why?"

"Because I've been married to him for the last twelve years."

The line goes silent for a moment. "Excuse me?" the man says.

Kathi explains that she did find her husband, Steve, in the photographs—but that the name associated with the pictures is Eric Wright.

"That's weird," Percy says. "Are you sure it's your husband?"

"He has less hair now," she says, "but it's him."

Percy says that, to his knowledge, no one from Exeter has heard from Eric Wright in more than a decade. But when he was in school, the kid was well-liked and popular.

"We all thought the world of him," Percy says. "He was fun, spontaneous—always had a smile on his face."

That sounds like my Steve, Kathi thinks.

The two converse for a few more minutes, speculating about how strange it is that they're talking about the same person yet know him by two different names. Kathi mentions that she's been to Exeter only once because going back there was so painful for Steve.

"I'm sorry to hear that," Percy says. "Why is it so painful for him?"

"I guess because of his parents' deaths."

Percy laughs uncomfortably. "Eric's parents aren't dead," he says. "I just saw his mom last week in the grocery store."

Kathi goes cold. "What?"

"Yeah," Percy says. "They still live in the same house where Eric grew up."

Kathi almost drops the phone. Her whole body has gone numb. The news of Steve's lies—his parents, his house, his name—has left her dumbstruck.

"He told me his house burned down," Kathi says, her voice trembling.

Percy chuckles lightly. "We must not be talking about the same guy."

Kathi has the yearbook in front of her, and there is no doubt that the boy in the picture is the man she married. Of that she is certain.

But she isn't certain of much else at this point.

CHAPTER 17

KATHI IS AS NERVOUS as she can ever remember being. She keeps pacing back and forth through the house, checking and rechecking the front window, waiting for Steve to pull up in the driveway. The yearbook is in a brown paper bag on the kitchen counter next to her. She isn't sure how she should talk to Steve about what she's found, but she's decided to confront him straight on. No beating around the bush.

No games.

She knows about his background with the CIA and his time in prison. She knows he's always wanted to keep a low profile. So although she would have preferred it if he'd been honest with her, she can at least understand why he'd use a different name.

But the lies about his parents' deaths and about their house burning down?

Those are lies she doesn't understand.

Those are lies that deceive only her.

She looks around at the house they own together, the nice wood-framed cabin a few miles out of town. When they'd looked for a place to buy, she'd been drawn to the giant stone fireplace, the oak beams overhead spanning the open space in the vaulted ceiling, and the wood paneling along the walls.

"It's homey," Steve said when they looked at it with the real estate agent.

It's more than that, Kathi thinks now. *It's home.*

But now everything about their home feels cheapened by the knowledge that their relationship is built on lies.

In the fading evening light, Kathi spots the headlights of Steve's pickup truck pulling into the driveway. She takes a deep breath and tries to control her trembling limbs.

Yet when Steve comes in, he takes one look at her and says, "What's wrong, honey?"

He has always been in tune with her feelings, and she's always loved him for that.

She thinks for a moment about skipping the confrontation. He hasn't seen the yearbook yet. She could toss it in the garbage and forget the whole thing. Pretend she never saw it. She was happy when she was ignorant, wasn't she? She's afraid that bringing this up with Steve now will upend her whole life. What if they're never able to get things back to the way they were?

I can't walk away from this, she thinks. *I've always insisted that we be honest with each other. I'm not going to compromise on that now.*

"Honey?" Steve says. "You're worrying me. What's wrong?"

"When were you going to tell me about Eric Wright?" she finally says.

For a fraction of a second, Steve's expression falters and Kathi sees that her words have caught him off guard. But then his mask goes back on.

The liar's mask he's worn for their whole marriage.

"Who?" Steve says.

"Don't lie to me," Kathi pleads. "Not now. I've always thought our relationship was built on honesty. Please, don't lie to me anymore."

Steve squints, studying her. He looks serious—the smile is gone.

"What's all this about, Kathi?"

She reaches into the paper bag and pulls out his yearbook. She holds it up so he can see the cover.

"I wanted to surprise you for our anniversary," she says. "I felt bad that you didn't have any pictures from when you were a kid."

Seeing the yearbook, Steve laughs and steps forward to look at the book.

"That's sweet," he says, acting as if everything is going to be okay.

"You can imagine my surprise," she says, opening to the bookmarked page with Steve's—or Eric Wright's—senior picture, "when I found a different name next to your face."

Steve looks at his own photograph with an amused expression, his face still twisted into a half grin.

"Kathi, my love," he says, "I told you I was on the run. I told you the CIA was looking for me. You didn't really think Steve Marcum was my real name, did you?"

Kathi hates the way he's talking to her, the condescending tone of an adult speaking down to a child who has just made an immature conclusion about something beyond her comprehension.

"I guess I could have told you, but what good would it have done?" he says. "I don't feel like I am that person anymore. The boy in that picture might be Eric Wright, but I'm not. I'm Steve Marcum."

Kathi feels tears coming to her eyes. Steve has always been able to sweet-talk her, and she's afraid she's going to fall for it again this time.

"Okay, so I didn't tell you that name," he says, "but I was honest about where I came from. I could have lied about that, too. I probably *should* have lied about it. You ought to be flattered that I was so honest with you."

"But you weren't honest, Steve," Kathi says, unsure whether she should even call him Steve anymore. "You lied about your house burning down. You lied about your parents dying. I don't know what to believe anymore."

In an instant, Steve's expression turns from entertained to glowering.

"What did you do?" he asks, his voice almost a growl, his eyes burning holes into her with his expression.

"I talked to an old classmate of yours," Kathi says defensively. "He teaches at the high school now. When we realized we were talking about the same person, I was pretty embarrassed that I didn't know my own husband's name."

"Did you share the name Steve Marcum?"

"Yes."

"Did you tell him where we live?"

"I gave him our address," she says. "He had to send the—"

As quick as a snake, Steve's hand flies to Kathi's neck and grabs her throat in a vise grip. He shoves her hard, slamming the back of her head into the refrigerator. Magnets and photos from the fridge go flying. Tiny bursts of light dance across Kathi's vision. She tries to say his name, but no words leave her mouth.

And no air comes in.

The path for oxygen has been completely cut off.

CHAPTER 18

WITH HIS HAND ON HER THROAT, Steve glares at her, his eyes narrowed, teeth clenched. He looks like a monster.

How could I ever kiss this man? Kathi asks herself. *How could I make love to him?*

She claws at his arms and flails her feet, but to no avail. He lifts her by her neck until she has to get on her tiptoes in order to touch the floor. He's stronger than she ever realized, holding her pinned against the fridge, her feet straining to find the ground below her.

In a panic, she thinks, *I've married a killer, and now he's going to kill me. This is what I get.*

Then he releases her, and she drops to the floor, gasping, crying. The magnets and photographs from the refrigerator are spread around her on the tile floor, mementos from all the places they've visited together.

Steve kneels down, breathing heavy.

"You brought this on yourself."

He tries to put a hand on her, but she twists away. He won't be denied. He grabs a fistful of her hair and makes her look him in the eye. He balls his other hand into a fist and draws it back.

"Listen here," he snarls. "Don't mention the name Eric Wright ever again. Forget you ever fucking heard that name. Do you understand?"

Kathi is paralyzed with fear.

She doesn't recognize the man staring at her. She realizes she's seeing Eric Wright—the real person hidden behind the mask of Steve Marcum—for the first time in her life.

Suddenly, he releases his grip on her and apologizes. His anger turns to despair, and he starts crying along with her.

"I just snapped," he explains. "You've got to understand that if the wrong people find out I'm here, I'm dead. And they'll probably kill you, too. Do you see why I'm so upset?"

But as Steve cries, Kathi finally sees through him. That night at the cemetery, he cried so hard that she believed there was no way he could be faking the pain. But it was all a lie—an untruth that had nothing to do with protecting himself from the CIA. If she could believe that his secrets and lies were all to protect himself from the wrong people finding him, she might be able to forgive what he just did. But he still hasn't offered an explanation for why he made up those stories. No explanation for why he broke down in that cemetery and sobbed. All that elaborate deception was just done to manipulate her.

To toy with her.

If those tears were fake, these ones are, too.

"I love you," he wails. "But you really fucked up."

"I'm sorry," Kathi says because she knows that's what he wants to hear.

"Can you forgive me?" Steve says, tears streaking

his cheeks. "I can't live with myself if you don't forgive me."

Kathi wraps her arms around him.

"I'm so sorry," she says. "I just want things to go back to the way they were. I forgive you. Let's just forget the whole thing."

Look who's lying now, she thinks.

CHAPTER 19

DIVORCE?" SARAH SAYS. "I can't believe it! What happened? Steve's such a nice guy, and you two seem so good together."

Kathi sits with her old friend in a bar in downtown Denver. Out the window, they can see Mile High Stadium under a brilliant blue Colorado sky. Inside the bar, the handful of other customers are shooting pool. Cigarette smoke hovers in the beams of sunlight coming through the window. A Rockies game is on the TV, muted. A Pearl Jam song plays on the stereo.

As the days count down toward her twelve-year anniversary with Steve, Kathi has done her best to make Steve—or Eric—think that everything is normal.

When Steve wants to kiss her, she offers him a quick peck.

When he wants a hug, she gives him one but is the first to break off the embrace.

When he wants to have sex, she politely declines.

"You said you forgave me," he says, trying to slide a hand up her blouse.

"I do forgive you," she tells him. "I just need time, okay? That was pretty traumatic for me."

"I understand," he says, pulling his hand away. "I'm sorry. I'll give you all the space you need."

She feels as though she's walking a fine line. She wants him to believe that she's still upset but working toward forgiveness. If she acted as though nothing happened, he wouldn't believe her. He knows her too well to think she'd let things go so easily. But she can't let on how truly angry she is, how hurt. The truth is, she can never forgive him. There's no going back to the way things were.

His touch makes her skin crawl.

His kisses make her want to scream.

The thought of having sex with him makes her want to throw up.

She has a meeting scheduled next week with a divorce lawyer, but she couldn't stand being around Steve until then, so she told him she was going off to spend the weekend in Denver visiting her friend Sarah. Steve looked suspicious, and she could see the gears turning in his brain. He clearly didn't want her to go, but if he said no, kept her on a short leash, that contradicted his claim that he'd give her space. So he didn't protest.

He did give Kathi a warning, however.

"I know Sarah is your best friend," he told her, "so if you want to tell her we're having a rough patch, I understand. But you can't tell her about all my secrets, okay? We can't let this get out."

As Kathi sips from her glass, she decides that she doesn't give a damn about keeping Steve's secrets. She needs to get them off her chest.

"Steve isn't who you think he is," Kathi tells Sarah. "Steve isn't who *I* thought he was."

She tells her friend everything: about his time in the

CIA, in prison, the lies about his parents and his home burning down. Sarah's mouth is wide open practically the whole time Kathi speaks, with one gasp after another coming from her lips.

Finally, Kathi pulls down the collar of her turtle-neck to show Sarah the purple bruises still on her neck from where Steve clamped his fingers around her throat.

"That son of a bitch," Sarah says, having done a complete 180 on the subject of Steve Marcum since the beginning of the conversation. "Not only should you get a divorce, but you need to get a goddamn restraining order!"

They order more drinks and talk over Kathi's options. Outside the window, the sun descends toward the horizon, filling the bar with warm orange light.

"You know, if his name isn't really Steve Marcum," Sarah says, "if his whole identity is fraudulent, you might not actually be married at all. You could probably get the whole marriage nullified or invalidated or whatever they call it."

Sarah also points out that if Steve doesn't want his identity outed, then Kathi can demand whatever she wants in the split.

"I actually think you hold all the cards here," Sarah says.

They discuss a plan: Kathi will tell her lawyer about how Steve used a fake name, but she won't reveal his real name—at least not yet. And she won't mention the CIA or prison or anything like that.

"I don't want to get the guy killed," Kathi says. "I just want him out of my life."

Sarah smirks and takes a sip of her beer.

"What?" Kathi asks.

Sarah shakes her head. "I don't believe for one

minute that Steve—or Eric or whatever the hell his name is—was ever in the CIA."

"Why not?"

"I think he's a compulsive liar who just wanted to get laid."

Sarah heads toward the bar to pay the tab. Alone, Kathi stares out at the setting sun, drinking the last warm swallow of her drink. Her friend is probably right. Has Steve been lying to her since the day they met? She tells herself she bought his stories because he always had an air of mystery about him, and that part wasn't a complete fabrication. After all, he came to Colorado with hardly any possessions to his name. He had no old friends at the wedding. No relatives. Not a single friend from before they met.

The son of a bitch is running from something. She's sure of that much. But if it isn't the CIA, what could it be?

As she watches the last rays of sunlight disappear over Denver, she vows to find out.

CHAPTER 20

KATHI SITS AT A MICROFICHE MACHINE at the Denver Public Library, scrolling through back issues of various newspapers. She's been at this for days. She called Steve and said she was having a great time with Sarah and planned to stay longer.

But what she's really doing is searching for Eric Wright.

She spent two days making long-distance calls to Exeter, California—racking up who knows what kind of phone bills for poor Sarah—and talking to school-teachers, the newspaper editor, and anyone she could find who remembered Steve. She couldn't bring herself to call Eric Wright's parents, but she did find out that Eric *had* served in Vietnam—*at least that much seems to have been true*—and, after returning, moved to the California Bay Area to become a police officer.

That information led her to the basement of the Denver Public Library, where she's been scouring old issues of the *San Francisco Chronicle* and the *Oakland Tribune*. She was afraid that the Colorado library wouldn't have Bay Area newspapers on microfiche or microfilm and was pleased to learn that it had an extensive archive of major newspapers. She doesn't know what she's looking for exactly, but Kathi figures that if Eric was a police officer, his name might pop up somewhere. After hours of searching, she eventually stumbles upon a brief about the youngest person ever promoted to lieutenant in the Alameda County Sheriff's Office: Eric Wright.

The background the article gives on him matches what she's learned so far. It says that Eric Wright served in Vietnam from 1968 to 1970 and then joined the sheriff's office. He became a lieutenant at the young age of twenty-nine, making the promotion newsworthy.

Despite this confirmation, Kathi can't imagine Steve as a cop. Wearing a uniform. Following orders. Sure, he's smart enough, driven enough, to have earned the promotion that the article mentions. That doesn't surprise her. But Steve isn't the kind of guy who does things by the book. He doesn't like to follow rules—she can't see him enforcing them.

Funnily enough, she *can* picture him as a CIA assassin. That rogue way of life seems more his style.

But it turns out that job was just another one of his lies.

As Kathi searches, she tries to investigate Steve's other story: that he served time in prison for manslaughter after a bar fight. She can't find anything about that, and as she scrolls through the weeks, closing in on the time in 1980 when she met him, she thinks she's not going to find anything.

But then something else catches her eye.

It's not a big article, not prominently featured, just a brief with a headline stating that the police called off the search for a missing Oakland man. The detective interviewed stated that the man, a former lieutenant in the Alameda County Sheriff's Office, had faked his own abduction. The man's name? Eric Wright. But it's the final sentence in the article that leaves Kathi chilled to the bone.

The article says that Eric Wright ran out on a wife and newborn baby.

And that he had two children from a previous marriage.

Kathi feels so nauseated, she has to sit back and take deep breaths. It sickens her to think that he was married before and never told her—and even worse, to know that he abandoned his children. Her skin is clammy. The contents of her stomach boil inside her like magma churning under a volcano. She closes her eyes and tries to calm herself to keep the vomit from erupting onto the microfiche console.

When the queasiness finally passes, Kathi puts her head in her hands and cries. She weeps long and loudly with no regard for other library patrons who might hear her. She is mourning the twelve years of her life that she spent with a man she never really knew.

Afterward, as she dries her tears, she feels thankful that she was able to find the information she did. She wanted to solve the mystery of Eric Wright. And now she has.

At least she hopes so.

She hopes there aren't more skeletons out there, waiting to be discovered.

CHAPTER 21

KATHI SITS IN THE BUSIEST restaurant in Glenwood Springs during the lunch rush hour, waiting for Eric Wright. She's decided to start thinking of him as Eric Wright, not Steve Marcum.

That will make what she needs to do today easier.

When he walks in, he tries to offer her his usual smile, but she can tell he's forcing it. He sits across from her.

"Hello, Kathi," he says.

"Hello, *Eric,*" she says, emphasizing his real name.

He makes a sour face. "Please don't call me that."

"It's your name, isn't it?"

"Not anymore."

"Did you legally change it?" she asks.

"Not legally," he answers, looking around and noting the crowded restaurant. He must know that she picked this restaurant and this time of day so there would be plenty of witnesses. "No one here knows me by that name. And I'd like to keep it that way. Please."

She doesn't respond, just stares at him with her lips pressed tightly together.

He looks down at the packet of paperwork lying on the Formica table between them.

"Is that what I think it is?" he asks.

She nods. He opens his mouth to speak, but the server approaches to take their order.

"Want your usual, Steve?" the woman asks.

"Yes."

"Kathi?"

"Nothing for me," she says. "I won't be staying."

As the server leaves, Eric stares at Kathi with a pleading expression.

"Please, Kathi. Don't do this. We can work it out. I want to work it out."

Kathi wishes that were possible. She wishes she could go back to the life she had. The life she's known for the past twelve years. It's hard to give up. She misses skiing with her husband. Soaking in hot springs together. Going on hikes and camping trips. Mornings on their back deck, drinking coffee and enjoying the view of the Rockies rising up over the mist in the meadow behind their house.

It all seems so comfortable and nice—so romantic—but she knows that life is over. It's already been destroyed. Now that she knows the truth, she can't go back to her old life.

"I don't want to get divorced," Eric says.

"We're not," Kathi says, "since we were never actually married."

She explains that because he didn't use his real name, their marriage isn't legally binding. Therefore, the documents she wants him to sign will simply invalidate the marriage. As long as he doesn't make the separation difficult, she promises not to drag him through a contentious court battle where she tells everyone in town his real name.

She slides her diamond engagement ring and wedding band off her finger and lays them on the table. Eric pockets them quickly, looking around to make sure no one has noticed.

"Please don't do this," Eric says. "You're the love of my life."

"Did you use that line on your first wife?"

Eric's sad face turns to stone.

"Or your second?"

Eric takes a deep breath and sits back in his chair, crossing his arms. "So you know about that, huh?"

Kathi nods gravely. "Technically," she says, "you're still married to your second wife."

"What else do you know?"

Kathi gives a tight smile. This might be the first time in their relationship that she's been the one with the upper hand, and not the other way around.

"You ran out on three kids," she says. "No wonder you didn't want anyone to find you. You weren't afraid of the CIA. You were afraid you'd have to pay child support. They're probably all teenagers by now, aren't they?" Kathi huffs aloud and says, "'Most Dependable,' my ass."

Eric takes another deep breath, clearly angry but trying to hide it. He looks around, reminding himself of all the bystanders in the restaurant.

"Careful," Kathi warns. "There are witnesses this time, *Eric*." She emphasizes his real name, saying it loud enough that other people might hear.

Eric leans forward, placing his elbows on the table. He cracks his knuckles, first one hand and then the other.

"Okay, Kathi," he says. "I'll let you go."

"You'll let me go?" she snaps. "You don't own—"

"Go on and live your own life," he says, interrupting

her. "But before you walk away, I want you to listen to something. Don't keep digging up dirt about me. And don't tell anyone what you know about me. This is your only warning."

His eyes look so dark, so evil. How could she not have seen it before?

"You think you're clever, finding out a few things about me?" he says. "You don't know a goddamn thing. You don't know who I am, what I've done. There are people out there who will make trouble for me if they know I'm here." He leans even closer, boring into her with his paralyzing gaze. "If they make trouble for me, I'm going to make trouble for you."

Kathi tries to maintain his stare, but she's terrified. Tears are welling in her eyes.

"Do you understand?" he asks menacingly. "I want to hear you say it."

Kathi hesitates. She doesn't want to be intimidated by his threats, but the truth is she's scared of the man sitting across from her.

"Here you go, hon!" says the cheerful voice of the server as she plops a plate of steak and eggs in front of Eric.

As if a switch has been flipped, he transforms in an instant from a frightening and intense brute to the charming, happy-go-lucky gentleman everyone in the community knows.

"Thanks so much," he says, smiling and spreading a napkin across his lap, as if he and Kathi have been talking about something as innocuous as the weather.

Kathi uses the distraction of the server to make her escape, but she's only about three steps away when Eric calls out, "Oh, Kathi," almost singing the words.

Reluctantly, she turns to face him.

"We had some fun, didn't we?" he says, beaming with the same magic smile she fell in love with.

"It doesn't matter," she says. "All those memories are ruined now."

Eric shrugs and lifts a knife and fork to dig into his steak.

Looking at him, she realizes that he feels no sympathy for her, no empathy—no normal human emotion. He can't understand how he's hurt her.

Or he doesn't care.

"I shouldn't have too much trouble finding a replacement for you," he tells her matter-of-factly. "But you won't find anyone as fun as me. I can promise you that."

"You know, Eric," Kathi says loudly enough to attract looks from fellow patrons, "I see you for who you really are. You're nothing but a scared little boy who's afraid no one will like him, so he lies about who he is. I pity the next person who falls for your scams, but it damn sure won't be me."

With that, she spins on her heel and struts out of the restaurant, holding her head high.

CHAPTER 22

Fall 1993

KATHI SPIARS CAN'T SLEEP. She notices that the blackness outside her window is starting to turn blue. It's nearly dawn, and she's pretty sure she hasn't slept a wink.

She rises from her bed, wraps herself in a flannel robe, and descends the stairs to the living room. The weather has been pleasant for this time of year, but it's still Colorado, so the house is cold first thing in the morning. She boils a kettle of water to make herself a cup of herbal tea. When it's ready, she steps out onto the back deck and watches the world slowly come more and more into focus. Clouds cling to the peaks of the blue mountains. In the meadow before her, a herd of elk move without a sound through the morning fog, their silhouettes like phantoms in the morning light.

It's been months since the separation, and Kathi is a mess.

She's willing to admit that to herself.

It doesn't help that Eric is still around. She thought he would move out of Glenwood Springs—on to his next adventure—but apparently he plans to stay. She's passed him driving down the street. She's seen him at the grocery store. She heard from a client that he got fired from his job for saying something inappropriate. Someone else told her that he was working as a masseur now, going to people's houses to give massages.

Their old friends can't believe Kathi and Steve split—"You two were perfect together!" they all say—and Kathi has been tight-lipped about what led to their breakup. She thought it would make it easier if she didn't gossip behind her ex's back, but actually, it's only made her feel alone.

She got the house, her business, all the physical things that meant anything to her. But she's still grieving for what she lost.

She lost her husband, and her best friend.

The fact that Steve was an illusion doesn't help matters. In fact, it only makes it worse that the man she loved turned out to be a mask and the real person underneath such a lowlife. She's embarrassed that she could've been duped so easily. She's ashamed at her gullibility. But grieving the end of the twelve-year marriage and suffering emotionally from the betrayal aren't the only reasons she lies awake at night.

She can't help but think that there's more to Eric Wright.

He's running from something more than a couple of ex-wives, a few kids, and years of missed child support payments. She's sure of it. Now that she no longer thinks he worked for the CIA, she has a feeling the reality is something much simpler.

Eric always included some truth with his lies. He did serve in Vietnam. That was true. And he did grow up in Exeter. He even drove her to the city. He could have made up any city in California, any city in the country, but he actually took her to his real hometown.

It was as if he needed a grain of truth to make the lies convincing.

Sure, the CIA story was BS, as she assumes was the claim that he went to prison for getting into a bar fight. But maybe there was a grain of truth to those tall tales. Maybe he really did kill someone—just not as a hit man for the CIA and not in some bar fight. Maybe faking his own death wasn't just to run out on his wife and family responsibilities.

Maybe he killed someone and ran away so he wouldn't get caught.

When he talked about murder, he was always very convincing. Of course, he was convincing in all his lies, but she has the added experience of having looked into the man's eyes when he had his hand around her throat. In that moment, she certainly believed he was capable of murder.

It sounds far-fetched, but she just can't shake the feeling that Eric Wright is getting away with something.

As Kathi sips her tea and lets the sun warm her, she thinks about what she can do. She's not a cop. She's not a private detective. What can she do?

But she remembers her dogged determination while scrolling through issues and issues of old newspapers on microfiche. Maybe she *is* the right person to look into the past of Eric Wright. She probably knows him better than anyone now. She knows the fake Steve Marcum, and she knows the real Eric Wright.

If she's not the right person to look into his past, who is?

Kathi rises from her seat on the deck and stares out at the meadow behind the house. The sun peeks over the distant mountains and bathes the landscape in bright orange light. The silence begins to awaken with birdsong.

Kathi feels better than she has in a long time.

You messed with the wrong girl, she thinks, staring at the sunlight bathing the morning in gold. *You'll regret the day you ever lied to me.*

PART 3

CHAPTER 23

Winter 1994

DETECTIVE JOHN LUCAS of the San Joaquin County Sheriff's Office sits at his desk on his lunch break, eating a Jack in the Box fried chicken sandwich with curly fries. As he dips a cluster of fries in ketchup and pops them into his mouth, his phone rings, the red light flashing with an incoming call.

He swallows the bite and answers, "Detective Lucas."

"John, this is Tracy from the front desk," a familiar voice says. "We've got a woman on the line from Colorado who wants to know about unsolved murders from 1980."

"Nineteen eighty?" he says, quickly doing the math in his head. "That was fourteen years ago."

"You were around back then, weren't you?" Tracy asks. "Would you mind talking to her?"

Lucas consents and takes a sip of root beer before the call is transferred. Most of the time, calls like this turn out to be wild-goose chases. But Lucas tells himself to have an open mind.

"Detective Lucas," he says when the call is put through. "How may I help you?"

The woman identifies herself as Kathi Spiars from Glenwood Springs, Colorado, and says she's spent the past few months calling every law enforcement agency within a hundred miles of Oakland to ask about unsolved murder cases from 1980.

"Most of the officers haven't taken me seriously," she admits. "I hope you will."

"I'm listening," Lucas says, eyeing his sandwich and wishing he'd been able to finish it before taking the call. He's been starving all morning.

The woman on the phone says that she met a man in October 1980 and fell in love with him. He was very mysterious, she says, claiming he'd been in the CIA and was on the run.

Lucas almost rolls his eyes. *This* is *a wild-goose chase,* he thinks.

The woman goes on to tell him that although they were married for twelve years, their whole relationship was built on lies. It turns out she didn't even know his real name. She explains that the man's real name is Eric Wright, and he was a former sheriff's lieutenant in Alameda County who faked his death and ran out on his wife and child, plus an ex-wife and two other kids.

"Did you talk to the ex-wives?" Lucas asks.

"Not yet."

"Did you talk to the Alameda County sheriff's office he used to work for?"

"They said they'd look into it," she says, "but I'm afraid they think I'm just some jaded woman with an ax to grind."

Detective Lucas can't blame them. He knows from experience that investigators are constantly overwhelmed, juggling cases and trying to find evidence—real, hard evidence. A detective has to look past the conspiracy theories to find facts. And some woman calling from several states away who's mad at her ex-husband is exactly the kind of time waster you have to tune out sometimes.

His stomach growls. The sooner he can end the call, the sooner he can go back to his sandwich. But there's no sense in being rude. The least he can do is listen to her and try to get off the phone without hurting her feelings.

"What exactly are you hoping I can do for you?" Lucas says as politely as possible.

"Honestly," she says, "I think he killed someone. I want to know about any unsolved murders from around that time. I was blind to who he really was for years, but now I see him clearly. I just have a hunch that he's done something really bad."

Lucas takes a deep breath and fills his cheeks with air before blowing it out. He explains that what she's asking isn't as easy as it might seem. The truth is that crimes—including murders—go unsolved all the time.

"What you have is a murder suspect and no crime to go with him," Lucas says. "That's not normally how we do things. Usually it's the other way around—we have the crime and we look for suspects. We can't simply go back through every unsolved murder from around that time and add him to the suspect list," Lucas explains. "That's not how it works. I'm sorry. We just need more to go on than a hunch that he did something bad."

She's quiet for a moment and then says, "I understand." He can tell by her tone that she's disappointed. He's just another person in law enforcement who isn't taking her seriously. Once again, she's getting nowhere.

"It's just," she starts, "this guy was so mysterious. I'm telling you, he's hiding something. He faked his own death. He changed his name. He hid gold bars in the toilet. He—"

Detective Lucas sits up in his chair. "What did you say?"

"Yeah," she says. "He faked his own death. There—"

"No, no. About the gold. What did you say?"

The woman says that Eric Wright—a.k.a. Steve Marcum—used to hide unmarked gold bars in their toilet tank because he was afraid the house might burn down and he wanted the precious metals to be safely submerged in water.

"I'm telling you, nothing about this guy was normal," she says, and when there's no reply from the officer, she asks, "Did we get cut off?"

But Lucas is there, lost in thought. At the mention of gold, his heart rate picked up and began galloping.

He remembers divers going into the canal outside Tracy to find a body that two fishermen spotted in the aqueduct. The scene is as clear to him as if he saw it yesterday. He might have forgotten a lot of faces, names, and facts in his two decades on the force, but he remembers all the dead bodies. You don't forget those.

This one was weighed down with a heavy chain, which kept the corpse submerged but able to drift slowly down current, making it difficult to determine where it had been dumped into the aqueduct. The body was in the water for weeks, its chest bloated with gas, the hands and feet swollen and wrinkled. The man's skin was pale white in some places, greenish black in others, and chunks of flesh were torn away where the chain had rubbed against the body, leaving gray gouges in the muscle. The smell was so rank, it was difficult not to vomit.

The body was decomposed enough that the medical examiner found the cause of death inconclusive.

But the police were able to identify the body—a man whose gold went missing after his death.

"Ms. Spiars," Detective Lucas says, "can you give me a phone number where I can reach you? I want to check on something and get back to you."

After he hangs up the phone, Lucas hurries out of his office, leaving the remainder of his chicken sandwich uneaten on his desk.

CHAPTER 24

DETECTIVE JOHN LUCAS WALKS through the dark shelves of the evidence storage facility, looking at case numbers on rows and rows of cardboard boxes. The boxes are covered in dust—everything in this row is more than a decade old. Lucas is alone in the quiet room, which is roughly the size of a basketball court. Each row has its own line of fluorescent tube lights, and Lucas has switched on only the ones in the rows he's searching, leaving most of the storage area in complete darkness. Cold air emanates from the concrete floor.

When he finds the case number he's looking for, Lucas pulls the cardboard box down off the shelf and walks to a desk in the corner. He sits under a pool of fluorescent light and opens the box.

This is the case for the unsolved death of a man named Lester Marks. The sheriff's office did its best to look into it, but the case soon went as cold as the corpse they pulled out of the aqueduct that August of 1980. As Lucas goes through the files—the crime scene photographs, the medical examiner's report, a pile of paperwork taken from Marks's office—the details of the case come back to him.

Lester Marks, fifty-seven, had been considered a small-time criminal in the area. He was a precious metals dealer, and police believed he worked as a fence for stolen jewelry, melting the pieces down into ingots and selling them. When police arrested him in 1979, they confiscated five hundred thousand dollars' worth of jewels and gold. Marks pleaded guilty to possession of stolen property but avoided jail time due to his heart condition. Among his collection were seven gold bars, each weighing two and a half pounds, that the police had no way of proving were stolen. They ultimately gave the gold back to him. A year later, Lester Marks was murdered.

The gold was never found.

At the time of his death, the bars were worth two hundred thousand dollars.

Sheriff's investigators always assumed that someone had killed Marks for his gold, but they were never able to figure out who. Now, as Detective Lucas reads through the documents in the folders, he searches for any potential connection between Marks and Eric Wright.

Unfortunately, he doesn't see any. And without a connection, he can't reopen a case that's so cold it's practically frozen in ice.

The fact that Eric Wright disappeared from California shortly after the murder is certainly intriguing. But the word of a woman in Colorado claiming that her ex-husband *used* to own gold bars is not enough. Kathi Spiars said the gold bars were long gone, so there's no way to compare them to the photographs in the case file.

Lucas scours the paperwork from Marks's old office: papers with handwritten notes about gold values, telephone conversations, some of them random phone numbers or dollar amounts with no context.

The detective's fingertips have gone black from handling the old documents. His stomach rumbles, and he's reminded of his uneaten lunch sitting back at his office. Yet something tells him to keep looking. The chronology and proximity of Lester Marks's death and Eric Wright's disappearance doesn't feel like a coincidence.

Lucas moves faster and faster, now only skimming the documents. He doesn't know what he's looking for but is sure he'll recognize it when he sees it.

His eyes pass over a document, and he almost flips it over to put on the pile of papers he's already gone through, but then he does a double take.

He lets out a long, relieved breath.

There it is, he thinks.

The name Eric Wright is scrawled in ink on a handwritten note taken from Lester Marks's office.

And there's a phone number next to it.

CHAPTER 25

KATHI IS ANNOYED. She spoke with that detective at the San Joaquin County Sheriff's Office three days ago and hasn't heard from him since. She believed him when he told her he was going to look into the case. But it turns out he was only trying to get her off the phone. At least the other cops had the decency not to give her any false hope.

But that guy, Detective Lucas, made her believe he might help.

She knows now that she has to keep digging. Kathi sits down at her kitchen table and sets the cordless telephone next to her. She'll badger every damn cop in California if she has to.

As she reaches to make her first call, the phone rings, startling her. She has a sick feeling that it's Eric, breathing heavy into the phone and about to say, *I heard you've been making calls about me, Kathi*.

She tells herself to relax and answers the phone.

"Ms. Spiars?" says a voice. "This is John Lucas with the San Joaquin County Sheriff's Office. We spoke on the phone a couple of days ago."

"I thought you forgot about me," Kathi says.

"Sorry, ma'am. I just wanted to look into this thoroughly before I called you back."

"And?"

Lucas pauses for what seems like ten seconds before saying, "Ma'am, I think you might be right about your ex-husband."

Waves of emotion pour through Kathi. Relief that someone has finally taken her concerns seriously, relief that she's not in this alone. At the same time, she's horrified to realize the kind of man she was married to. Sure, he always claimed to be a hit man—as preposterous as that sounds to her now—but he maintained that he'd killed only evil people and had committed those acts in the service of doing good. But the thought that she spent more than a decade sleeping next to a cold-blooded murderer feels different to her.

Before, she always told herself that Steve was a good person at heart.

Now she knows that's not true.

"What did he do?" Kathi says, her voice hoarse from her suddenly dry throat.

Lucas explains that a small-time crook was killed a short time before Eric Wright fled California. The man owned gold bars that the police believed were made from melted jewelry that had been stolen—but they couldn't prove it. Lucas searched through the old files and found the name Eric Wright scribbled on a note from the man's office. There was a phone number with it, and Lucas called it and reached a precious metals firm in the Bay Area. Lucas interviewed the owner and discovered that Eric Wright used to work there and that he'd previously been a sheriff's lieutenant.

"A note with a name and phone number is a pretty

flimsy piece of evidence," Lucas says, "but it prompted me to dig a little deeper." He goes on to tell Kathi that the son of the murder victim is currently serving time for armed burglary, and that he visited the man in prison.

"I asked him about Eric Wright," Lucas says. "He wasn't sure about the name, but he said his dad had been talking about selling the gold to a dirty ex-cop. Those were his words. *Dirty ex-cop.*"

Kathi is breathing fast. *We've got you, you lying son of a bitch,* she thinks.

I got you.

Lucas says that he feels it's possible that Eric Wright talked with Lester Marks and made arrangements to buy the gold on behalf of the company he worked for. But instead of buying the gold, he murdered Marks and stole it.

"When he left California, he might not have been running from the law," Lucas says. "He might have felt he got away with it. He might have seen the gold as the means to getting a fresh start. Maybe that was his motivation for the murder to begin with. The gold was his ticket out of there."

"So you're going to arrest him?" Kathi says, feeling triumphant.

"I can't arrest him," Lucas tells her. "Not yet."

"What do you mean?"

Lucas explains that the evidence linking Eric to the murder is tenuous at best: a scribbled note, the word of a convicted burglar, and Kathi's story that he once kept gold bars in the toilet. Everything else they know about Eric Wright certainly paints him in an unsympathetic light—the lies, the fake death, the way he ran out on his family—but none of that is damning evidence in the case of the murder of Lester Marks.

"Most of what we have is what they call circumstantial evidence," Lucas says. "We need real, hard evidence."

"Like what?"

"A murder weapon. Forensic evidence. DNA. Fingerprints."

"How do you get that?" Kathi asks.

"I don't know if I can," Lucas says, further deflating Kathi's balloon of hope. "The body was buried thirteen or fourteen years ago. If your ex still had some of the gold bars, that would help. But you said they're gone?"

"Long gone," Kathi says. The adrenaline high she was riding turns into stomach-twisting dread. "So what now? He's going to get away with murder?"

"I need to come to Colorado and interview him, see what he says," Lucas explains. "Maybe he'll slip up and tell us something we don't know. Maybe he'll confess."

"Fat chance," Kathi says.

"He might not see a way out."

"He always comes up with a new lie to explain his way out of things. That's what he does. He tells lies like the rest of us breathe air. It comes that natural to him."

"I think we'll get him," Lucas says. "This is the first step. You've done a good thing coming forward, Ms. Spiars."

Lucas says that he'll keep her updated on the status of the case, but in the meantime, she needs to steer clear of Eric Wright.

"If he finds out that we've been talking," Lucas says, "you could be in real danger."

CHAPTER 26

Summer 1994

DETECTIVE JOHN LUCAS STEERS his rental car through winding mountain roads. To one side, huge peaks rise up outside his window; they're topped with snow so thick it hasn't melted all summer. To the other side, the shoulder drops off in a steep cliff. No guardrail separates the rental's tires from a two-hundred-foot plummet.

The air is thin this high up, and Lucas feels a dizzying sense of vertigo. He can't help but be relieved when the road finally drops in elevation and the land begins to flatten out. Like Denver, where his plane landed, the town of Glenwood Springs is a mile above sea level, but it feels much lower now that he's driven through mountain passes of ten and twelve thousand feet.

Lucas drives directly to the local police station and is greeted by the police chief, a friendly middle-aged man with a mustache and an accent suggesting he's from Texas, not Colorado.

"Is he here?" Lucas asks.

"Yep," the chief says, hitching up his belt. "He came willingly. Didn't make a fuss. We put him in the interview room for you. He didn't bring a lawyer with him, although we informed him that was his right."

The chief leads Lucas into the back corridor of the station and points down the hall to the interview room. Lucas thanks him, and before they separate, the chief stops him with a gentle hand on his arm.

"Something you should know," the chief says.

Lucas waits. When he called the chief and asked permission to come into his jurisdiction to conduct an interview, he mentioned it was a murder case but gave the man no specifics. He didn't even say that Eric Wright—whom the chief knows as Steve Marcum—was the suspect.

Just that he was a person of interest.

"We brought Steve in about a month ago to question him about some forged checks," the chief says. "Between you and me, I'd say he's as guilty as sin, but we couldn't make anything stick. Had to let him go."

Lucas nods. Falsifying documents sounds just like the Eric Wright he's come to know through the investigation.

"Thanks for letting me know," he tells the chief.

"No problem. But that ain't why I'm bringing it up," the chief says.

He explains that when they brought Steve in that first time, before they officially started the interview, the man made an offhand remark that got the chief's attention.

"He comes in and says something like, 'What's this all about? Is California investigating me for a homicide? Did somebody find some bones in the water?'"

A chill climbs up Lucas's spine. If there was any doubt in his mind before that Eric Wright was guilty, there isn't now.

"He seemed relieved when he realized we was just

asking him about some check forgeries," the chief says. "Sure enough, he had a story for every one of our questions. When I asked him, on the record, about those bones he mentioned, he laughed and said he was just kidding. He's a slick one, that Steve Marcum...or whatever you said his real name is."

Lucas asks if the chief will sign a statement saying exactly what he just said.

"You bet," he says. "I'll go write it up right now as you're interviewing the guy."

Lucas and the chief part ways, and Lucas pauses outside the interview room. There is a one-way mirror allowing him to look in on Eric Wright, and he studies the man for a moment.

Eric Wright appears to be in his early to midforties, his hair thin on top and sandy blond on the sides. He seems to be in shape. He was probably quite lean through most of his adulthood but seems to be putting on a little weight now that he's crossed into the land of middle age. He's sitting back in the chair, his long legs stretched out under the table, his arms tucked behind his head, as though he's in a beach chair getting some sun.

Throughout his career, Lucas has seen plenty of people waiting in interview rooms like this, and they're almost always nervous—even the ones who don't need to be. They hunch over in their seats, trying to make themselves small, or they fidget. Or they visibly quiver. Or sweat an inordinate amount for the temperature in the room.

But Eric Wright looks as cool as can be.

Relaxed.

From where he's standing, Lucas can see Wright's profile, not his full face. But the detective would swear that the corner of the man's mouth is curled up in just the hint of a smile.

Detective Lucas takes a deep breath and enters the room to face Eric Wright—a man he knows has gotten away with murder thus far, and who looks confident that he will again.

CHAPTER 27

ERIC WRIGHT POPS TO HIS FEET as soon as Detective John Lucas enters the room, his expression friendly, his demeanor cooperative. He looks like a man who doesn't have a care in the world.

Lucas introduces himself and asks Eric to have a seat.

"You're a hard man to find, Mr. Wright."

Eric shrugs and smiles. "I guess the secret's out. My ex-wife must be running her mouth."

Lucas doesn't acknowledge this comment. It's important that he doesn't reveal that he and Kathi have talked—for her sake. He hopes his poker face is as good as Eric Wright's.

Lucas explains that the name Eric Wright came up in an old homicide investigation and that they traced the name to his hometown of Exeter, where someone said they heard he had changed his name and was living in Glenwood Springs, Colorado.

Eric frowns as if the whole situation is confusing to him.

"How can I help?" he says.

"Back when you lived in Oakland, did you know a man named Lester Marks?"

"Doesn't ring a bell."

"Not when you worked in precious metals?"

"No."

"Or when you were a lieutenant with the Alameda County Sheriff's Office?"

Eric shakes his head. "Not that I recall."

There are classic tells that police use in order to detect liars: the eyes darting up and to the right, excessive hand gestures, throat clearing, looking away, touching the face. But Eric Wright does none of these. He keeps his body still and his eyes fixed on Lucas. He's good at maintaining eye contact and seeming sincere, unafraid—like a man with nothing to hide. He knows how to lie not just with his words but also with his whole body.

Detective Lucas knows that Eric will try to lie his way out of this situation. There's no chance of getting him to confess. But he's hoping that Eric will slip up, either give up some clue that will help the investigation or say something that can be used to show his unreliability when the case goes to court.

Lucas asks questions about Eric's work in precious metals, why he quit the police force, his whereabouts in the summer of 1980. Eric is initially cooperative but finally asks, "What's all this about?"

Without mentioning his conversation with Lester Marks's son or what the chief just told him—and definitely not what he learned from Kathi Spiars—Lucas explains that a note with Eric's name and phone number on it was found in the files from Marks's office. When investigators followed up on the lead, they discovered that Eric Wright went missing shortly after Lester Marks's body was discovered. That prompted the police to become more interested in finding him.

"Look," Eric says, for the first time using his hands to emphasize his words, "it's possible I could have talked to this guy, whatever his name was. That was my job—I talked to people about buying gold. I can't remember all their names. I damn sure didn't kill him, though, if that's what you're thinking."

Lucas says he's just trying to explore every avenue of the case. He doesn't want to let on that, at this point, Eric is the only suspect.

"You have to understand why we'd want to talk to you," Lucas says. "You faked your own death, Mr. Wright. Would you care to explain why?"

"I didn't fake my own death," Eric says, looking defensive for the first time. "I can explain what happened, but you probably won't believe a word of it."

CHAPTER 28

ERIC WRIGHT LEANS BACK in his chair, as if settling in to tell a story. He reminds Detective Lucas of a storyteller sitting at a campfire, preparing to captivate his audience. He certainly has the air of someone who can tell a good story—and knows it.

Eric says that what happened was, he went to meet a man to buy precious metals. The deal sounded too good to be true, so Eric had the foresight not to bring any of the company's money with him.

"I thought I'd just go and test the temperature of the water," Eric says. "If the sale seemed legitimate, I would go back to my boss and ask for the funds."

"Was the contact Lester Marks?" Lucas asks.

"No."

"What was the person's name?" Lucas asks, holding his pen over his notebook, pretending he's ready to write it down.

"I don't remember."

"Then how do you know it wasn't Lester Marks?" Lucas asks.

Eric hesitates, as if he's walked into a trap. "Okay,"

he says, "I concede that it *could* have been him. I don't know. I don't remember the name. The name Lester Marks doesn't sound familiar. That's all I know."

Eric says that the rendezvous was in a motel in Richmond, California, in the East Bay area of San Francisco. When he arrived at the motel room, two men drew guns on him and then assaulted him when they found out Eric hadn't brought any money.

"They punched me, kicked me. One of them whacked me on the head with the butt of his gun. The last thing I remember is staggering out to my car and sticking the key in the ignition."

Eric says he next remembers waking up at a bus station in Colorado with a terrible headache and no recollection of who he was or where he lived. He had amnesia and couldn't remember his own name. However, he somehow had an ID that said his name was Steve Marcum.

"In the precious metals business, I used to have various fake names and IDs to go with them," he says. "It can be dangerous when you're dealing with gold—as I discovered myself that night. But when I came out of the blackness and found myself in Colorado, I had a big blank in my memory, so I just assumed my name was Steve Marcum. My picture was on the ID, for crying out loud."

"Did you have any money?" Lucas asks.

"Not a cent."

"No gold bars?"

Eric Wright's eyes narrow, trying to read the detective. "Who said I had gold bars?"

"Lester Marks owned gold bars that went missing after his death," Lucas says.

"Oh," Eric says, shaking his head and moving on. "Where was I?"

He claims that he started to get his memories back but by then he'd already started a life in Colorado. He'd met a woman named Kathi and didn't want to return to his family in California.

"Now if you talk to my ex-wife Kathi," Eric says, "she'll tell you that I made up some cockamamie story about working for the CIA. It's true—I lied. But that's because I really couldn't remember who I was back then."

By the time his past came back to him clearly, Eric claims, he and Kathi were already head over heels for each other.

"I couldn't very well tell her the truth," Eric says. "If I had said, 'Oh, by the way, I didn't really work for the CIA—I ran out on my family,' she would have been gone. I liked the sex too much at that point."

Detective Lucas isn't surprised that Eric has brought up Kathi in order to preemptively discredit her. He speaks as though he's confiding in Lucas, as though they're locker-room pals. *You're a fellow man,* his tone seems to suggest. *You know the lengths we go to in order to score with women*. The way Eric talks about his ex-wife disgusts Lucas, but the detective realizes that's probably the point. Lucas doesn't have to like him. He just has to believe him. And if he doesn't believe him, at minimum Eric needs to tell a story that won't come back to haunt him if the investigation continues.

"She's a looker," Eric says.

"You told your ex-wife you worked for the CIA?" Lucas says, trying to sound surprised by this admission to keep up the pretense that the two haven't talked. "And she believed you?"

"I know, it's ridiculous," Eric admits. "But Kathi ate it up. I told her all kinds of crazy stuff. That my parents were dead. That I killed people for the CIA. That I went to prison. It seemed like the bigger the lies I told, the crazier she was about me. Not the sharpest tool in the shed, that one."

She was smart enough to lead me to you, Lucas thinks.

CHAPTER 29

KATHI IS SITTING ON HER back deck, looking out over the meadow, when she hears a car pull up in the gravel lane leading to the house. Fearing, as she always does, that it might be Eric, she quickly peeks around the corner of the house to see who it is.

A nondescript car pulls up and parks, and out steps a man in a police uniform. It's different from the one the police in Glenwood Springs wear, beige instead of dark blue, but he's definitely a cop.

"May I help you?" she asks, coming around the corner.

"Kathi Spiars?" he asks.

"Who wants to know?"

"I'm Detective John Lucas with the San Joaquin County Sheriff's Office in California."

Lucas extends his hand to shake hers, but instead Kathi rushes forward and embraces him.

"Thank you for believing me," she says.

"Thank *you,*" he says. "Without you, we wouldn't even be looking at Eric Wright."

Kathi invites Lucas in and puts a kettle of water on

the stove for tea. Lucas sits with her at the kitchen table and explains that he just interviewed Eric Wright.

"How'd that go?" she asks.

"You were right," Lucas says. "He lies like he breathes air."

"So can you arrest him?"

Lucas says his next step is to take the case to the grand jury in San Joaquin County, which will decide if charges should be brought against Eric. The grand jury can subpoena Eric Wright and compel him to testify. Lucas cautions Kathi that this could take a while—and he needs to do more investigating before he's ready.

"Did you mention me in the interview?" Kathi asks.

"I didn't," Lucas says, "but he did. I think he underestimates you. Although if this investigation continues, he may start to worry about what you know, so you need to be very careful."

Detective Lucas says that he would like the names and contact info of anyone who could corroborate anything that Eric Wright—a.k.a. Steve Marcum—did that might be incriminating.

"Especially the gold," Lucas says. "Do you know anyone else who ever saw the gold before he sold it off? Or do you know where he sold it?"

Kathi says he never kept her in the loop. Every once in a while, she would sneak a peek in the toilet and see that there was one bar fewer. Eventually, she opened the toilet one day in the late 1980s and all the gold was gone.

To her knowledge, he used the money from the gold on himself—or for extravagances like vacations they took together. The house and her business were in her name, and none of the money from the gold was used for down payments on either. It was a source of pride for Kathi that she never needed a handout from her then husband to achieve her dreams.

"He was so hung up on me not marrying him for his money that I made sure I never benefited from it," she says. "If anything, he leeched off me over the years. I never really thought about it that much until we were divorced, but that's what happened. He hitched his ride to my wagon and rode it as long as he could."

Detective Lucas thanks her for the tea and rises to leave. Kathi walks him to his car, and before he leaves, he says, "One more thing. Did he ever mention having PTSD from his time in Vietnam?"

Kathi shakes her head no.

"Depression? Nightmares? Anything like that?"

"No," Kathi says. "Nothing bothered him. He walked through life like he was playing a game and was always on the winning team. Why?"

Lucas says that at the end of the interview, Eric mentioned that he had post-traumatic stress disorder from Vietnam. He theorized that it had contributed to what he called "a psychotic fugue state" during his disappearance.

"He said that after your divorce, he learned a lot about himself," Lucas says. "But I think he was trying to manipulate the conversation so he would come across as sympathetic."

"It's a scam," Kathi says with certainty. "I don't know what he's up to, but he's trying to work some kind of angle. You don't believe him, do you?"

"I didn't believe a word that came out of his mouth," Lucas assures her before climbing into his rental. "But it's not about what I believe. It's about what I can prove."

CHAPTER 30

Summer 1995

KATHI IS AT THE DESK in the salon, trying to ignore the Ace of Base song playing over the speakers and concentrate on making phone calls. Most of the calls she makes are dead ends, but she's trying to leave no stone unturned, as they say. Eric's parents won't speak to her, but Kathi talked to Eric's former employer at the precious metals company, associates from the sheriff's office he used to work for, employees at the BART station where his car was discovered. She's talked to all their old friends in Colorado to see if he ever slipped up and said anything relevant. She's gone back through their old phone records from when they were married and called every number she didn't recognize. She's contacted practically every used-jewelry store and pawnshop in Colorado to find out if anyone remembers a man fitting Eric's description selling gold bars.

She needs to find out everything she can about Eric Wright.

She needs him in jail so she can get on with her life.

Her long-distance phone bills, both here and at home, have gone through the roof, but she doesn't care.

As the Ace of Base song ends and the Elton John song from that Disney cartoon about lions begins—a slight improvement, Kathi thinks—the phone rings. She quickly answers it, hoping it's a callback.

"I know you're having a lot of fun playing private investigator," says the unmistakable voice.

The hair stands up on the back of Kathi's neck.

"What makes you say that?"

"This is a small town, Kathi. You've been running your mouth about me, telling people that my name isn't really Steve Marcum, that I'm dangerous."

It's true that Kathi hasn't been particularly secretive about her ex's past. When they first separated, she kept quiet, but lately she's been telling anyone who will listen about what a charlatan the man she used to be married to turned out to be—though most people haven't taken her seriously. They think she's just a scorned woman looking to smear his name. But Kathi feels it's her duty to warn people.

"Eric," she says, "you need to leave me alone. Stay out of my life."

"I swear to God, Kathi, if you don't stop this, you'll be sorry."

"Oh, yeah?" she says. "What are you going to do?"

There's a long pause, and Kathi wonders if he's tempted to threaten to do to her what he did to that guy in 1980. Instead he says, "Remember that night when you first discovered the name Eric Wright? I could have ended you right there. Just turned out the lights."

"You come anywhere near me, and I'll—"

"I don't have to come near you," Eric says. "Remember that deer we had mounted in the living room? I shot that at four hundred yards. Hunting season's coming up. You live next to the forest. I'd hate for there to be an accident."

"I'm calling the police," Kathi says, her voice hoarse with terror.

"Go ahead," he says. "See who they believe. Everyone here thinks you're some crazy bitch who can't move on with her life."

Kathi doesn't answer.

"If you leave me alone," Eric says, his voice suddenly more tender, almost caring, "I'll leave you alone. Understand?"

He waits for her to respond. She wants to say something tough, to sound strong, confident. But she's afraid her voice will come out timid and weak.

"I'll take your silence as a yes," he says, and hangs up.

Kathi sits there, her body shaking.

"Everything okay?" one of her stylists asks as she uses a broom to sweep up the hair on the floor.

Kathi takes a deep breath and tells her that yes, everything is fine. Then she picks up the telephone and resumes her investigation.

CHAPTER 31

Fall 1995

KATHI IS RAKING HER BACKYARD, doing some overdue maintenance on the lawn. She's trying to pile the leaves onto a tarp so she can drag them away. She's breathing heavily from working in the cold. Each exhalation comes out in a visible white cloud.

She takes an exasperated breath and looks around at how much more work needs to be done.

She's been neglecting everything about her home lately. The lawn is thick with pine needles and leaves. Branches lie strewn about from the last windstorm. The rosebushes needed to get trimmed this summer but she never got around to it. Her ex used to help her with this stuff; now he's the reason she's fallen so behind on it. She uses all her free time to dig into his past. It's a time- and energy-consuming endeavor, and the effort she's put into it has taken its toll on her.

The house isn't the only thing that needs maintenance. Business at the salon is suffering because she's been letting the place run on autopilot.

But she can't stop.

All Kathi thinks about is the investigation. She can

now understand why police work takes so long. It's been more than a year since Detective Lucas came to Colorado to interview Eric, yet he says he still doesn't have enough to take the case to a grand jury.

She'd be more frustrated with him if she wasn't seeing firsthand just how hard it is to conduct an investigation. She scours newspapers, makes phone calls, flies to California to interview people who knew Eric. She tracks down old police reports to search for other crimes that might be associated with him. Almost every road is a dead end, but once in a while, she'll find a nugget of information that will open a new avenue of inquiry. It's all she can do not to drop the rake right now and go back inside to keep looking.

Come on, she tells herself. *These leaves won't rake themselves.*

As she bends over and drags the rake through the brown grass, the loud crack of a rifle report makes her jump. Her heart pounds in her chest, and her limbs fill with adrenaline.

It's not unusual to hear gunshots—it's that time of year—but she can't recall ever hearing one so close to the house.

She looks out into the forest, trying to spot the orange of a hunter's vest. Then, as if floodgates are opening, more gunshots split the air in rapid succession. She flinches and ducks her head.

A high-speed whirring noise zips over her head, like a bumblebee flying a hundred miles an hour.

Oh, my God, she thinks. *That was a bullet!*

Another one flies just a few feet over her head.

"Stop shooting!" she screams, waving her arms in the direction she assumes the shots are coming from. "Stop!"

The shooting ceases, and in the silence afterward,

Kathi hears only her own panicked breathing. She stares out at the meadow behind her house and into the woods beyond.

There is no sound.

No movement.

"There's a person here!" she yells. "Don't shoot anymore, asshole!"

She takes a cursory look at her house to make sure none of the bullets have hit it. Then she heads inside to calm her nerves. She has a drink of water and starts pacing around the house.

She wants to believe the bullets were coming from someone, far out in the woods, unaware that a house was along the trajectory of his shots. But now that she has time to really think about it, she can't believe it.

She's no expert on guns, but these shots seemed loud enough to have been fired within close proximity to the house. And no hunter actually interested in hitting what he was aiming at would fill the air full of lead like that.

She remembers Eric threatening her about not needing to get close to cause "an accident." Her eyes move toward the deer mount. After the separation, Eric didn't want his hunting trophy and she never bothered to take it off the wall. But she stares at the empty space underneath the deer head.

When he moved out, Eric did take his rifle.

CHAPTER 32

San Joaquin County, California
Fall 1997

DETECTIVE JOHN LUCAS STEPS into the courtroom, where the grand jury has convened. The judge's chair sits empty, but the jury box is filled. Lucas is sworn in by the bailiff and takes a seat in the witness box. This is not his first time testifying in a courtroom, nor his first time testifying before a grand jury, but for some reason he feels more nervous than usual.

The case is old and it's strange, so he's not sure what the grand jury will make of it. But more than that, Lucas feels that what he's doing is important. Eric Wright has gotten away with his crimes for far too long.

It's time to bring him to justice.

Lucas tells the whole story of Eric Wright—everything he knows about him, anyway. He constructs a narrative based on all the information he has. He doesn't try to spin the facts. There are enough pieces of evidence—the scrap of paper, the gold bars, the statements from Kathi Spiars and Lester Marks's son—for him to create a likely narrative of Wright's actions and motives.

As he talks, Lucas studies the members of the grand jury. Some seem skeptical. Others look surprised. All are riveted by the story—they've never heard any criminal case quite like this.

Faked his own death?

Stole gold?

The CIA?

And she believed him?

"It sounds like the plot of a movie," the foreman says finally.

Lucas can't argue with that.

The foreman turns to the bailiff and asks if Eric Wright has been subpoenaed. The bailiff informs him that a subpoena was delivered but that Mr. Wright hasn't arrived at the courthouse yet.

"Do we have any idea if he's on his way?"

The bailiff shakes his head no. Then all eyes from the jury turn toward Lucas, every member registering what this might imply.

"Excuse me," Lucas says. "I need to make a phone call."

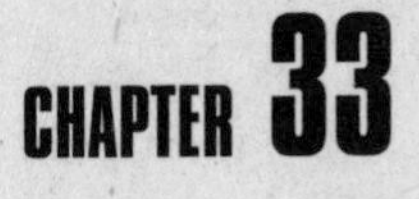

CHAPTER 33

KATHI SPIARS IS CHANGING a display in the salon's front window, rearranging bottles of shampoo and humming along with the new Jewel song playing on the speakers. She's in a good mood, knowing that the grand jury in California is finally hearing the case.

Years have passed since she first called Detective Lucas, and two alternating concerns have occupied her life since. The first is an obsession with finding out everything Eric Wright did, every ounce of evidence that might be used to prove he is a thief and a murderer. The second concern is an all-consuming fear. She's been gripped with crippling anxiety that Eric Wright will come after her to put an end to her search for the truth. Despite the fact that she changed her locks long ago and installed an alarm system, Kathi still has trouble sleeping at night, afraid that she'll wake up to his hands on her throat. Whenever she tries to sit peacefully on her back deck, she fears bullets flying across the meadow.

She's thought many times about selling her house and her business and leaving Glenwood Springs. But now that the case is going to the grand jury, she hopes that won't be necessary.

Maybe her days of being afraid are almost over.

Detective Lucas told her it would be unlikely that the jury would arrive at a decision for at least a few days. So when the phone rings, Kathi lets the stylist who's flipping through a magazine at the front desk answer the call.

"Kathi, it's for you," the stylist calls out after a few seconds. "Some cop from California."

Kathi tries not to feel anxious about the call. *He's just calling to give me an update,* she tells herself.

"How did it go?" she says when she has the phone, trying not to sound too nervous.

"Well, I've got good news, bad news, and really bad news."

Kathi's heart sinks. "What do you mean really bad news?"

"Eric Wright's in the wind," he says.

"In the wind?" Kathi says, unfamiliar with the expression.

"We think he's run off," Lucas says. "Again."

Kathi feels ill. Her legs go weak, and she has to sit in order to keep from collapsing. Her shaking hands struggle to hold the phone to her ear.

When Eric Wright didn't show up at the grand jury hearing, Detective Lucas called the Glenwood Springs Police. They went to his residence and found his apartment cleared out. They checked with his landlord, who said Eric hadn't been there for the past two weeks. Two weeks ago would've been about the time he received the court summons.

"Goddamn it," Kathi mutters, tears springing to her eyes.

He's going to get away with it, she thinks. *That crazy lying maniac is going to get away with murder.*

"It's not all bad news," Lucas says.

"Did they issue an indictment?" Kathi says, hopeful for at least a silver lining.

"No," Lucas says. "That's the other bad news. The grand jury didn't think there was enough evidence to pursue charges. But they did say that they thought I was onto something. They encouraged me to keep digging."

Kathi struggles to see this as a silver lining.

"I've been working on this thing in my spare time," Lucas explains. "Now I can actually open the investigation. We can interview anyone who ever met Eric Wright or Steve Marcum. We'll find more evidence."

Kathi is deflated. "What does it matter?" she asks. "He's gone. Hell, he could be in Canada by now."

"He got away before because no one was looking for him," Lucas says. "Once I can issue an arrest warrant, he'll find it a lot harder to keep a low profile. We'll get him. It's just a matter of time."

"How much time?" Kathi says, unable to keep her tears at bay. "It's already been three years." It's been years already, yet Lucas is saying that the investigation is only now going to officially *begin*?

Lucas apologizes for the fact that the wheels of justice turn so slowly. As always, before he hangs up, he encourages her to be careful.

"You okay, Kathi?" one of her stylists asks when she hangs up the phone, lost in thought, remembering Eric Wright's hand around her throat, pushing her against the refrigerator. The look on his face as he was seconds away from killing her.

Kathi's voice cracks when she says, "I was thinking it's time for me to leave Glenwood Springs." She turns to her employee. "Know anyone who wants to buy a salon?"

December 1997

KATHI STANDS ON HER BACK DECK—or what used to be her back deck; the sale of the home has just been finalized—and looks out over the meadow one last time. Part of her is sad to leave this house. But because she shared it with Eric, part of her is also glad to say good-bye to it.

She'll miss this view, though. That's for sure.

The meadow is covered in snow, gleaming in the sunlight as if sprinkled with glitter. Animal tracks crisscross the white landscape, and a breeze blows snow snakes across the frozen surface. A lone hawk circles the meadow, gliding through the blue sky. Kathi takes a deep breath of icy air and feels the cold scorch her lungs.

She's going to miss the air, too—the crisp coolness of it.

She's not yet sure where she'll end up, but she's thinking someplace warm. She doesn't know where in the world Eric Wright is now, but if he comes back to Glenwood Springs looking for her, he'll find no trace of her.

In the past few months, Kathi has sold her business, auctioned off most of her belongings, and sold the house that she once thought she would grow old in. She's crammed everything she has left into her Ford Explorer. Once she gets where she's going—wherever that is—she'll sell the SUV, too, and buy a new vehicle.

And there's something else she plans to change: her name.

Kathi is aware of the irony that she was married to a man who changed his identity because he was on the run, and now she's changing *her* identity because she's on the run from *him*.

She's vowed that until Eric Wright is behind bars, she's going to stay in hiding. She told Detective Lucas that she'll check in with him periodically and let him know where she is, but she plans to keep her whereabouts a secret from everybody else. She can use calling cards and pay phones to reach friends and family without telling them her location. They might think she's being paranoid, but they didn't see the look on her ex's face that day when she first called him Eric Wright. They still think he's probably harmless. *Sure, he told tall tales,* people have said, *but we never believed his stories anyway.*

"You didn't really believe him, did you, Kathi?" some old friends have asked, shaming her for being blind to his deceptions.

My eyes are wide open now, she thinks.

Kathi heads to her driveway and climbs into her SUV, fires up the engine, and drives away. The tires crunch noisily over the snow covering the driveway.

Tears blur her vision as she wonders how long it will be before she can come back to Colorado.

An undisclosed location
April 28, 2002

KATHI SPIARS—now known as Betty Hoffman—slides a DVD into her player and sits back on her couch to watch the film. She rented the movie from the Blockbuster Video that's within walking distance of her trailer. It's some car racing movie called *The Fast and the Furious,* which sounded entertaining enough. It was between this and *A Beautiful Mind,* but she figured the recent Oscar winner would be too heavy. She just wants something mindless to distract her from her thoughts for a couple of hours.

Before the movie begins, she sits through the trailers for upcoming new releases. One of them makes her sit up on her couch—*The Bourne Identity*. She laughs, remembering reading the book way back when she and Steve were dating, long before she knew the truth about him.

God, was that really twenty years ago?

I can't believe it. How time slips by.

For years, Kathi beat herself up for ever trusting Eric Wright. But she's learned to cut herself some slack. She was young and naive. She wanted to believe that the man she loved was some kind of cool spy.

The reality turned out to be something far worse.

And definitely *not* cool.

Ever since leaving Colorado, Kathi has been bouncing around the United States, never staying in one place for very long. She stretched her savings about as far as she could and worked various odd jobs under the table to make ends meet. For the past six months, she's been living in this trailer park, serving drinks down the street at the local VFW.

Twenty-two years after meeting Eric Wright, she's back to serving drinks and listening to drunk men flirt with her. The only difference is that back then she was turning the heads of twenty- and thirty-year-old guys with money to burn. Now she catches the eye of seventy-year-old World War II veterans who sip a single beer over two hours and leave a twenty-five-cent tip.

When she's not working, Kathi rents movies from Blockbuster, reads books from the library, or goes for long walks in nature. Mostly, though, she spends her time teaching herself to be a detective. She spends hours at the library doing internet searches, or on the phone digging up whatever she can about the man she used to be married to. She requests county records and court transcripts and police reports. She uses what little money she has to fly to California to conduct interviews.

She found out that shortly after their separation, Eric Wright forged her signature to buy a minivan, which explained what wrecked her credit for years.

She found out that Steve's former wives' names both began with a *K*—Kate and Kristy—and that both were petite blondes, just like her.

She found out that Eric's alias, Steven Marcum, came from a death certificate he bought illegally. The real Steve Marcum died as a baby the same year Eric was born, making his identity a suitable one to steal. Equipped with a real Social Security number from a deceased child, Eric was able to fabricate a new identity that looked legitimate to government agencies, employers, and banks, not to mention to Kathi herself.

Pretty much none of what she's found out has matched up with the kind, caring man she thought she was married to.

Sometimes she pulls out the Exeter yearbook and looks at the boy who would grow up to become the liar, swindler, and murderer she now knows him to be. She imagines him as a teenager realizing that he didn't experience the same kinds of emotions other people did. Realizing that he lacked empathy—cared nothing at all for the feelings and well-being of others. She pictures him practicing how to manipulate people: how to lie believably, to cry on cue, to be the puppeteer pulling the strings of those around him.

Did he always think only of his own self-interest and self-preservation, never concerning himself with the pain of others he left in his wake? Or was that a skill that he honed as he grew into adulthood?

Kathi bought a cell phone a year ago, which makes it easier for her to keep in touch with Detective Lucas—now a lieutenant—and share whatever new information she's found. She sometimes wonders if he's just humoring her by taking her calls. Has he given up hope? He has other cases to occupy his thoughts.

But there are no other cases for Kathi.

On the screen, a beautiful young actress is crying because the handsome blond man she's fallen in love with has turned out not to be who he seemed. Kathi is only remotely aware of what's happening in the film. Her mind drifted away minutes ago. She can't seem to take her mind off her mission.

Her obsession.

She pauses the movie and goes to the bathroom. She catches a glimpse of herself in the mirror and, as she often does, wonders where the adventurous young woman she used to be has gone. She doesn't think she looks too bad for a fifty-two-year-old who's been in hiding for years. She's still got a good figure for a woman her age. Sure, she's got some wrinkles and age spots, but she knows how to make the most of her makeup. And she has her health. Besides her feet and knees aching after a long shift, she feels quite good for someone who's walked the earth for half a century.

Still, Kathi laments wasting the best years of her life on a liar.

When she returns to the couch, she doesn't turn the movie back on. Why bother? Since she left Colorado, not a day has gone by that she hasn't thought of Eric Wright or the mess he's made of her life. She tries not to be bitter. But it's hard when she knows he's out there, who knows where, doing who knows what. She doubts he thinks about her half as much as she thinks about him. Probably not even a fraction as much.

Her cell phone rings.

The first thing she wonders when she answers, as always, is whether she'll hear Eric Wright's voice on the other end. It doesn't make logical sense. There's no way he could get her number. But still she feels that initial fear every time her phone goes off.

She tells herself not to be afraid and flips open the phone.

"Betty Hoffman speaking," she says, using her latest alias and trying to keep her voice steady.

"Kathi," Lieutenant John Lucas says, unable to hide the excitement in his voice, "I have news. We know where he is."

Guaymas, Mexico
April 29, 2002

ERIC WRIGHT WALKS ALONG the beach on the Sea of Cortez in Mexico. Holding a pair of flip-flops in his hands and wearing a droopy sun hat to cover his scalp, he walks close to the water's edge so that when wavelets wash ashore, the lukewarm water splashes his ankles before retreating back into the ocean. The bay, an incredible cerulean color, is full of boats coming in and out of port. The smell of salt water fills the air.

Guaymas is a port community for shrimp fishing and industrial shipping. It's positioned where the Sonoran Desert meets the sea, creating a sharp contrast between the dry desolate earth and the brilliant blue of the ocean. Some tourists visit Guaymas for its sports fishing opportunities, but it's not nearly as crowded with visitors as nearby San Carlos, with its expansive beaches and fancy hotels. Guaymas flies under the radar, as they might say in America.

And that's what Eric likes about it.

He turns from the beach and heads toward the street. Before stepping from the sand onto the pavement, he drops his flip-flops and slides them on. He's a little out of breath. Physically, Eric Wright is not what he once was. He's over fifty years old, and Father Time has finally caught up with him. The thin, athletic man has been replaced by an overweight, hunched-over version of himself who is more out of breath shuffling through the dirt roads of this sea-level Mexican town than he was when he once hiked the high peaks of the Rocky Mountains. He knows he's the one to blame for his slide toward flabbiness. Besides his daily walks along the beach, he isn't particularly active, certainly not the way he once was.

Life has become a bore.

He subsists on a two-thousand-dollar monthly check from the United States. It turns out Uncle Sam is as gullible as his ex-wife. Ever since he filed the disability paperwork claiming he had PTSD, he hasn't had to work at all. For a while, he thought about running a few scams: forging traveler's checks, buying over-the-counter medication and telling Americans it was some miracle drug that they can't get in the U.S., duping tourists to pay up front for fishing expeditions and then disappearing before the trip (he wouldn't even need to own a boat). But he quickly realized that any of those scams would draw too much attention to himself. And besides, two thousand dollars a month goes a long way down in Mexico.

As he walks among the adobe buildings, children coated with dirt and sweat crowd around him, offering to sell him gum. He waves them away. He could teach these kids a thing or two about making a living. There's always a scam and someone willing to fall for it—whether it's a government agency or a young woman looking for love.

Back at his apartment, he kicks off his flip-flops, grabs some leftover quesadillas from his tiny refrigerator, and eats them cold while sitting up in bed. The window air conditioner blasts cool air directly onto him. He picks up the remote and scans the channels. He doesn't understand half of what anyone is saying. His Spanish has become proficient enough to get by, but he's still far from fluent.

Outside his window, over the sound of the TV and the whir of the air conditioner, he can hear the bustling activity in the streets: children laughing and yelling, men and women bartering, cars zipping up and down the road, their engines whining. All of it blends together in a comforting white noise, and Eric finds himself getting sleepy.

He stretches out on the bed and lets his eyes drift closed. He falls into a dreamless sleep.

When he wakes up, he can tell from the sunlight coming through the window that a significant amount of time has passed. He feels groggy. It was one of those deep naps that it's hard to climb out of. But even though he tells himself it's just that he's not quite awake yet, something feels off.

The noises outside—the kids yelling, the adults arguing, cars driving by—are all gone except for a few distant voices outside.

It's too quiet.

Eric rolls out of bed and crouches—he curses himself for letting his belly grow so big—and strains to reach under the bed. Feeling a little paranoid, he grabs the duffel bag that he keeps hidden under there; it's filled with money, a few changes of clothes, and all the documents he needs to start over somewhere else. His motto has always been to err on the side of caution, and that philosophy has kept him safe all these years.

As he rises to his feet, a terrible crash against his apartment door makes him flinch. Wood splinters around the handle, and the door clatters inward. Uniformed men follow, shouting at him in Spanish and aiming rifles and pistols at his chest. Eric doesn't need to be fluent in Spanish to know what they're saying.

He's under arrest.

Eric drops the bag and puts his hands in the air. He isn't scared. He can talk his way out of this. Or bribe his way out. Or promise a favor of some sort. This is Mexico, after all. Aren't all the cops corrupt?

He can tell from the uniforms that this is the Policía Federal Preventiva—the national police force—and not the local cops. Still not a problem. They can be paid off with money or favors just like anyone else.

A man in a white tie and sport jacket pushes through the police holding a bundle of paperwork in one hand.

How can he wear that suit in this heat? Eric thinks. *I'm sweating my ass off in shorts and a T-shirt.*

"Mr. Wright," the man says in unaccented English, "do you understand what is happening to you?"

"Whatever it is," Eric says, "I'm sure we can work something out."

He smiles at the man to show him that he understands how this works and is willing to make an arrangement. He's confident in the power of that smile. He's been winning people over with it all his life.

The man looks at him seriously and pulls a badge out of his jacket and shows it to Eric. The letters FBI are clearly visible.

Eric's smile disappears.

I guess that explains why he doesn't have an accent, Eric thinks.

He realizes for the first time that this might not go his way after all. He assumes they found him because he used his real name when collecting his government disability checks. He had to. Steve Marcum never went to Vietnam—Eric Wright had to be the one to claim PTSD. It was careless, but honestly, he didn't think they would bother to track him all the way here. Eric figured Kathi and that cop from California would give up eventually. He certainly didn't think they'd get the FBI involved.

The FBI agent puts away his badge and holds up the packet of papers he was carrying when he walked in. It's actually three different documents that he shows to Eric one by one.

"This is your arrest warrant from the United States," the FBI agent tells him. "And this is your arrest warrant from Mexico. And these"—he holds the final document close to Eric's face so he can see it—"are your extradition papers. You're going back to the United States, Mr. Wright. Tonight."

CHAPTER 37

San Joaquin County, California
July 30, 2002

YOUR HONOR, the prosecution calls Kathi Spiars as its next witness."

Kathi walks into the courtroom, and all eyes turn to her. Except for those of the defendant. Eric Wright keeps his back to her as she walks past rows of people. In a weird way, she's reminded of her wedding day—walking through a crowd with all eyes on her, Eric at the end of the aisle—only this time, instead of a tuxedo, he wears a red jumpsuit with the word JAIL stenciled on the back.

The courtroom is crowded with journalists, including reporters from major news outlets. Once the details of the case came out—not to mention the fact that the wife of the killer was a big reason for his capture—the national media couldn't resist.

As Kathi walks past the defendant's table, Eric looks up. He doesn't smile, not with his mouth, but there is a twinkle in his eye. It's not a hostile look that he gives her, but something more playful. As if he's a good sport after losing a hand in poker—but maybe he still has an ace up his sleeve.

Time has changed him. His hair has grown darker and thinner on top—although he hasn't given up using the comb-over technique—and he's put on quite a bit of weight. He's thicker all around, and his once chiseled jawline sits atop a flabby neck. He's not particularly handsome anymore, if he ever was.

But he still has the same expression she always saw on his face, the same mischievous look, even if he isn't smiling with his mouth. The look unnerves her. She expected him to be humbled. Frightened, mad, forlorn—to show something other than this same look saying, *Isn't this all a big joke?*

Her legs feel weak as she raises her right hand and swears to tell the truth and nothing but the truth, so help her God. Her voice wavers at first, but as she gets through the oath, it grows stronger.

She's looked forward to this moment for years. Kathi relishes the chance to finally get out everything she has to say about Eric Wright—to get it all on the record.

This is the preliminary hearing in the murder of Lester Marks. There is no jury, only the judge, and the hearing is to determine whether there's enough evidence for the case to go to trial.

"Ms. Spiars," the district attorney, Thomas McGowan, says, "do you know a man named Eric Wright?"

"Yes," she answers.

"And how do you know him?"

"I was married to him for twelve years," she says. "He went by a different name back then, but he's the same person."

"Do you see him in the courtroom today?"

"Yes."

"Would you point him out?"

Kathi lifts her arm and aims her index finger at the man she once thought she would spend the rest of her life with. He looks back at her with a smirk on his face and a twinkle in his eye.

The expression seems to say, *I told you marrying me was going to be an adventure, didn't I?*

June 3, 2003

KATHI WAITS IN A CONFERENCE ROOM inside the district attorney's office. With her is Lieutenant John Lucas. They both have paper coffee cups sitting in front of them, but they've long since drained the contents.

They've been waiting longer than they expected.

Kathi arrived in San Joaquin County today for the start of Eric's trial, only to find out that the DA and Eric's defense lawyer were in a meeting.

It's been almost a year since the judge agreed to bind the case over for trial, but, as Kathi has learned time and again, the wheels of justice move slowly. She's had to wait for her opportunity to testify in front of the actual jury that will decide Eric's fate.

She felt good after her testimony at the preliminary hearing. She was able to lay out everything that happened and everything she did to investigate the real Eric Wright. Her former husband's mood changed as she spoke. The glint in his eye changed to a glower as he realized just how responsible she was for his arrest.

She was glad she could finally wipe that smirk off his face.

When she was told to wait in the conference room with Lucas, Kathi assumed the DA, Thomas McGowan, wanted to chat with her about her testimony. But now, as she waits for the DA to return, doubt begins to consume her. It might be that Eric Wright's luck hasn't run out after all.

The longer she waits, the more worried she becomes, and the more certain she is that he's going to cut a deal.

When McGowan enters the room, he is apologetic for making them wait.

"First of all," he says, "I just want to say that you've both done a phenomenal job. This case is two decades old, and Eric Wright wouldn't be in custody today if not for you." He looks at Lucas and says, "Top-notch police work, John." Then he turns his attention to Kathi. "You should be very proud, Ms. Spiars. This man would have gotten away with this crime if not for your tenacity and perseverance. You never gave up. As far as I'm concerned, you're a hero."

"I sense a *but* coming," Kathi says.

The DA takes a deep breath. "But," he says, "the case isn't strong. The preliminary hearing last year exposed the holes in it, and there's nothing we've been able to do in the last year to patch those holes. I'm going to let Mr. Wright plead guilty to voluntary manslaughter in lieu of a trial."

Kathi doesn't think that sounds so bad. "He'll still go to jail, won't he?"

"Yes, but the maximum sentence is six years. He could be out in two with good behavior."

Now Kathi feels sick. Only two years? For killing a person? For all the pain he's caused so many people?

Two measly years behind bars before he gets to go free again?

McGowan explains the problems with the case. There's no doubt that Eric Wright is a bad person: a compulsive liar, a deadbeat who ran out on his children, a fraud who fooled people into believing he was someone he wasn't. They can prove that all day long. But he's not on trial for those offenses—he's on trial for killing Lester Marks. And when it comes to killing Lester Marks, there isn't much hard evidence.

The case is so old that some of the evidence—Lester Marks's clothes, the chain that weighed down his body—has gone missing over time. The initial medical examiner's report was inconclusive, and there's no way to do another.

The note with Eric's name on it, Eric's comment to the police chief in Colorado about bones in the water, and even Kathi's claim that he kept gold in the toilet are all circumstantial.

Moreover, the defense attorney is suggesting that Lester Marks's own son probably killed him and is looking for a scapegoat. The father and son had a long, well-documented history of conflict, and the younger Marks has been in and out of incarceration his whole adult life. At best, the son is an unreliable witness; at worst, his history allows the defense an opportunity to craft an alternative narrative that could plant seeds of doubt in the minds of jurors.

On top of that, Eric's defense lawyer is trying to paint his client as a victim, making him out to be a long-suffering, traumatized veteran caught up in a case he has nothing to do with. Hearing this makes Kathi angry. Pretending to be a wounded veteran trivializes the suffering of real victims. Though of course for Eric

Wright, that's just another offense in a long list of shameful deceptions.

"I'm worried that if I go forward with the murder charge," McGowan says, "his lawyer might be able to get him acquitted. He might do no time at all. This way, we at least get him to admit to killing Marks. This way, he at least has to do *some* time behind bars."

"He has to admit it?" Kathi asks, realizing for the first time that this is what she really wants.

She wants her ex-husband to finally admit what he's done.

"It's an admission in a legal sense," the attorney explains. "He can still tell the judge that he didn't do it, but as far as the law is concerned, he is admitting to the intentional killing of another human being."

Kathi feels as though she's going to throw up. He doesn't even have to admit he's guilty. He can plead guilty yet maintain he's doing it for his own self-preservation.

"Please excuse me," she says, and she rises and walks out of the room, down the hall, and finds a large window overlooking a grassy area outside.

She stares out, not really registering what she's looking at. She's lost in thought. All her hard work—all these years of her life—has come down to this. *Was it worth it?*

A few minutes later, Lieutenant John Lucas finds her in the hallway.

"I always said it would be out of my hands once it got to this point," Kathi tells him. "Whether Eric got the death penalty or life in prison or only two years, that part is out of my hands. I know in my heart I've done everything I could."

Lucas agrees—there's nothing more she could have done.

"This has consumed my life for far too long," she says. "It's time for me to be done with it. It's time for me to wash my hands of it."

Lucas asks her what's next for her.

"I'm going to move back to Colorado," Kathi says. "I'll stick around for the sentencing, and then it's time for me to get on with my life."

CHAPTER 39

June 6, 2003

ERIC WRIGHT WEARS an ill-fitting suit to the sentencing hearing. The fabric sags on his now-bloated frame.

Kathi sits in the back of the courtroom, watching the proceedings. When it's Eric's chance to speak, he tells the judge that he has agreed to plead guilty to avoid the possibility of spending the rest of his life in prison. The judge explains to him, as the DA previously explained to Kathi, that for the purposes of the law, he is admitting to purposefully killing another human.

"I hereby sentence you to the maximum: six years in prison," the judge says. "And I order you to pay fifty-five thousand dollars to the family of Lester Marks in the form of restitution."

Fat chance of ever getting that money from him, Kathi thinks.

When the judge smacks his gavel down and everyone in court rises, Eric is all smiles. He shakes his lawyer's hand, beaming like a man who just got the best news of his life.

And maybe he did.

Kathi has made her peace with what she knew was going to happen, but still, it's a bitter pill to swallow. He didn't get away scot-free, but it's pretty damn close, as far as she's concerned.

The journalists in the front row begin to file out, some asking if they can get a statement from her when she exits the courtroom. She agrees to speak to them, but she's not ready to leave yet.

She watches Eric, who glances into the gallery and spots her in the back of the court. He keeps his eyes on her for a few seconds, nodding to her and offering a half smile.

It's only a look, a simple acknowledgment, but in her mind, the expression on his face says a lot.

It says, *You can't win them all. Maybe we both won a little and lost a little today.*

It says, *Whatever it was we had—the love, the hate, the hiding and the running—it's all over now.*

It says, *Not bad, kid—you're the one who caught me.*

Or maybe it doesn't mean any of those things. Smiling was always Eric's fallback expression, his ability to knock people off their guard, break down any hostility toward him—charm them. Maybe the expression has no meaning whatsoever.

Kathi gives him the slightest nod of her head. She isn't sure what she means to communicate with it—maybe just *Good-bye*.

Eric turns to the jail deputies waiting to take him into custody. As he disappears into the passageway to the jail, Kathi thinks—hopes—that this is the last time she will ever see him.

Kathi leaves the courtroom to find television crews ready and waiting for her, their cameras set up and their reporters brandishing microphones.

"Ms. Spiars, can we get a statement?" one says.

"Ms. Spiars, are you happy with this verdict?"

"Kathi," another asks, "is it true that today is your anniversary?"

Kathi squints at the woman asking the question. *My anniversary?* It dawns on her what the reporter is suggesting. It takes a moment to remember what day it is and whether it holds any significance for her.

"I hadn't realized," she says with a laugh. "Yes, twenty-two years ago today, I married a man and vowed to spend the rest of my life with him. But it turned out the man I married was not who I thought he was. They say love is blind—I guess I was blinder than most."

The reporters laugh and keep the cameras rolling.

"What's next for you?" a reporter asks.

"Now," Kathi says, taking a big, relieved breath, "I can finally say good-bye to this chapter of my life and move on."

EPILOGUE

Silt, Colorado
January 26, 2008

KATHI SPIARS DRAWS BACK the curtain on the front picture window of her two-bedroom home and takes a look at the snow falling outside. She turns off the light inside so she can see outside better. Her yard and neighborhood are blanketed in white, and more fat flakes rain from the sky. It looks as though there's no end in sight to this storm.

She doesn't mind. She has nowhere to be on a night like this. She turns the light back on, keeping it dim, and feeds another log into her wood-burning stove. She stretches out on the couch, pulling a blanket over her legs, and turns on the TV. She flips through the channels, trying to find something worth watching.

She stops when she spots one of the Jason Bourne movies playing. She considers giving the movie a chance, but the scene on the screen shows Matt Damon making an impassioned speech about being an ex-assassin running from his past, and the woman, that pretty German actress whose name she can't remember, is falling for him. Kathi begins flipping through channels again. She doesn't need to see an actor pretending to be a spy—she lived it.

After Eric's sentencing, she moved back to Colorado, opting for the small town of Silt, which is just twenty minutes down the road from Glenwood Springs. She loves this area of the state but couldn't bring herself to live in the same community where she has so many memories.

The district attorney, Thomas McGowan, called her a few years ago to let her know that her ex had been paroled and was free again. Since then, she's tried not to worry about him showing up to seek retribution. But sometimes, when there's an unexpected knock at the door, her anxiety looms—she fears it'll be Eric, not the mail carrier delivering a package. Or if she's out hiking alone, she sometimes worries that she's being followed. If a man appears on the path in front of her, she feels her breath catch in her throat until she can see his face clearly.

These fears evaporate as quickly as they appear, but she can't quite shake them completely. It bothers her that she can't entirely let go of the fear that gripped her for so many years. She's in her late fifties now, and she wants to make the best of what's left of her life, and not have the residual effects of her life with Eric Wright haunt her any longer.

Her cell phone rings. Having traded her old flip phone for a new smartphone, she can check the screen to see who is calling. Even though it's completely irrational, she always fears that she'll see the name ERIC WRIGHT.

Instead it's a number she doesn't recognize from Stockton, California.

She's not in the habit of answering calls from unknown numbers, but given where it's coming from, she has a feeling it's either John Lucas—now the assistant sheriff—or district attorney Thomas McGowan.

It turns out to be the latter.

"I've got some news that I thought you might want to know," the DA tells her. "Eric Wright is dead."

Kathi is not sure how to react to this. The news leaves her feeling numb.

McGowan explains that he got a call from a newspaper reporter in San Diego County who told him Eric Wright died of a heart attack at home with his wife.

"Apparently he remarried," McGowan says.

Of course he did, Kathi thinks. *I wonder if she was also a petite blonde with a name that started with* K, *like the rest of us. Or if he wasn't so choosy at sixty and just picked the easiest mark he could dupe.*

"The thing is," McGowan says, sounding nervous about delivering the next part of his news, "apparently the body has already been cremated. I actually feel a little skeptical about all this. Is it possible he faked his death again?"

Kathi's numbness turns to nausea. She should have seen this coming. Nothing in the life of Eric Wright was normal—of course his death wouldn't be, either.

"It's probably true," the DA says. "But given who we're talking about, I can't help but feel some uncertainty that everything is as it seems."

"I wouldn't put it past him," Kathi agrees, her mouth dry.

After they hang up, Kathi sits on her couch, lost in thought. While she would never wish for a person to die—not even Eric Wright—she has in many ways been looking forward to the news of his death. She always thought that if and when he died, she might be able to finally move on. She might finally feel safe again.

Goddamn you, Eric. You couldn't even give me this.

You couldn't even give me the peace of mind of knowing you're dead.

She realizes she'll spend the rest of her life as she has the past few years: mostly healed. Mostly unafraid. But always with those moments when there's a knock at the door or a voice in the woods, and her first thought will be, *He's finally come for me*.

She won't run again. She won't hide. The fear will never go away, not fully—but she can refuse to give in to it.

Kathi rises from the couch and again looks out the window at the snow falling outside. But because she didn't turn out the light, when she draws back the curtain, she sees nothing but blackness through the glass.

For all she knows, Eric Wright could be on the other side, staring back at her.

RAMP UP TO MURDER

JAMES PATTERSON

WITH MAX DiLALLO

PROLOGUE

April 10, 1991

SITTING ON A GUNMETAL-BLACK Yamaha Banshee ATV, idling on the shoulder of a sleepy desert highway, Robert Lyon removes his sunglasses and blots the perspiration from his brow. It's nearly 4:00 p.m., but the sun still feels blazingly hot—and the khakis, long-sleeved shirt, and bulky helmet he's wearing aren't doing him any favors.

Robert squints as he looks out at the barren, windswept landscape all around him. Shell Canyon, as the area is known, lies just outside Ocotillo, California. This tiny speck of a town sits about eighty miles east of San Diego and a stone's throw from the U.S.-Mexico border. With nothing but sand and craggy rocks as far as the eye can see, the place could almost pass for the surface of the moon.

"Ready to ride, squirt?" he asks.

Robert turns to David Lyon, his ten-year-old son, who is sitting on a smaller four-wheeler beside him.

"Almost!" David answers excitedly, fiddling with the chin strap of his oversize headgear. "This is gonna be awesome!"

Robert beams. He knows how much his boy has been looking forward to going ATV-ing. And so has he. While his wife and daughter are spending the afternoon lounging by the motel pool, Robert has carved out these few hours from his family's vacation to do some bonding, man to man, with his young son. To share some quality time together. To cut loose and have a little high-speed fun.

"Okay, Dad, I'm ready!" David declares. He revs his vehicle's engine. He's practically bouncing in his seat with anticipation.

Robert replies, "Now remember what the guy at the rental shop said. Accelerate slowly. Brake gently. And turn widely. You don't want to flip over. Any questions?"

"Just one." A sly grin creeps across David's face. "Think you can catch me?"

Before Robert can respond, his son jams the throttle and David's ATV roars to life. It lurches forward, kicking up a plume of sand and gravel.

Robert shakes his head good-naturedly. He engages his own throttle. And they're off.

Father and son are soon tearing across the wide-open desert flats, leaving a thick cloud of dust and exhaust in their wake. They rumble across a parched riverbed. They rattle through shallow canyons. They crunch over petrified tree branches.

David briefly glances back and flashes his father a smile as bright as the morning sun. He's clearly having the time of his life. He also seems to be gaining confidence in his driving—and gaining speed. Robert's paternal instinct is to call out to his son to slow down, to be careful, to take it easy. But he knows that over the whistling of the wind and the screeching of the engines, his words will never be heard.

Suddenly, as they pass a small ravine, David does slow down.

Then he banks so sharply to the left, looping back in the direction they came, that his side wheels briefly lift off the ground.

Robert watches, with confusion and concern, as his son completes this odd maneuver. He again has the fatherly urge to yell out to David, this time to ask what he's doing, to make sure everything's all right. Instead he applies his brakes, loops around, and follows.

As the haze of sand and smoke starts to dissipate, Robert sees that David has brought his ATV to a stop beside the ravine. His son is sitting motionless, staring at something. His head is cocked slightly to one side.

Robert slows his sputtering vehicle and pulls up a few yards away from his son, whose body and ATV are blocking Robert's view of whatever it is David is gawking at.

"Hey!" he cries. "David, you okay, pal? What happened?"

David slowly turns to face his father. His radiant smile has been replaced by a heartbreaking look of fear, shock, and bewilderment.

His voice shaky, David answers, "I…I saw it when we were riding by. I had to stop."

"Saw what? What is it?"

"Bones. Like the ones in my science textbook. Are they…*real*?"

Robert chuckles. He dismounts his ATV and walks over.

"Aw, squirt, bones are nothing to be afraid of. It's totally natural. Snakes, jackrabbits, coyotes—all kinds of animals live in the desert. And sometimes—"

"No, Dad," David interrupts. "Look."

Robert is finally close enough to see.

"Oh, my God!" he gasps.

He covers his mouth. He staggers backward.

There, lying faceup in the sand, is a perfectly preserved *human* skeleton.

Its limbs are extended, its knees and elbows bent at unnatural angles.

Its mouth, missing most of the upper front teeth, is wide open, as if frozen in an eternal scream of terror.

To a non–medically trained eye like Robert's, it's impossible to tell how long the skeleton has been lying out here. At what age the person died, or how. Even whether it's a man or a woman.

Stumbling backward to his ATV, overwhelmed by the awful sight, Robert knows only one thing for certain.

"We gotta get back to town," he says, "and call the police!"

CHAPTER 1

1986, five years earlier

KICKFLIP TO FAKIE. *Backslide hurricane. Anchor grind to noseblunt stall. Then end it with a sick ollie 360.*

"Yo, Gator, you fall asleep or something?"

Mark Rogowski opens his emerald-green eyes and smirks. He wasn't sleeping at all. He was thinking. Planning. Visualizing.

But turning to his friends Christian Hosoi and Tony Hawk, two fellow lanky skater boys standing at the edge of a massive outdoor half-pipe course, he jokes, "Yeah. I was dreaming, too. About your *mom*."

As his pals crack up, Mark hops onto his board, tilts it over the ledge, and plunges down the steep, semicircular ramp.

In a flash, he's zooming up the opposite side, his long auburn locks fluttering. At the top of the ramp, he goes airborne, twirling his board beneath his feet like a tornado before landing on the concrete again with a loud slap.

Mark shoots right back down the ramp and up another side. He catches more air now, going nearly horizontal, and flips his board around in a wild blur.

Back down and up the ramp he goes. This time when he's at the top, Mark slides his board a few feet along the ledge, balancing on it as if he were surfing a concrete wave. Then he slows to a stop and hovers, precariously, over the edge for a few tense seconds, seemingly defying the laws of gravity.

Now comes his big finish. Mark careens back down and up the half-pipe a final time, crouching low to maximize his speed. When he reaches the upper ledge, he soars to his highest height yet. He effortlessly spins not just his skateboard but his entire body around in midair, twice, before sticking a perfect landing.

Mark again rides gracefully back up the opposite ramp. He steps casually onto the same ledge he started from and tops off his performance with a faux-modest bow.

Tony, nodding with respect, gives him a congratulatory jab on the arm.

Christian claps his hands with vigor. "Dude, Gator, that run was sick!"

But Mark can barely hear him over the roar of the adoring crowd.

Gathered all around the perimeter of this sunny beachside skate park in Del Mar, California, is a mass of teenage fans, boys and girls screaming their adolescent heads off. Hundreds of them. Maybe thousands. Which, for a sleepy coastal suburb just outside San Diego with barely five thousand residents, is a pretty big deal.

That's because Mark "Gator" Rogowski is a pretty big deal, too.

He's a whiz at this new style of skateboarding known as vert (short for vertical), marked by dazzling, death-defying tricks performed on half-pipes, in empty swimming pools, and at custom-designed skate parks. Vert got its start right here in SoCal. But this new extreme sport—as well as its edgy, antiestablishment counterculture—is fast becoming the coolest, most popular thing on the planet.

And tall, trim, model-handsome Mark is one of vert's undisputed young superstars.

Along with Tony, Christian, and a few other homegrown skaters, Mark has built a massive young following. They're pushing skateboarding to new heights. Literally.

Not to mention the fact that they're cashing in. Many are teens themselves yet have started signing lucrative endorsement deals with clothing companies and equipment manufacturers. The more they grow their fan base, the more they earn.

Mark turns to the crowd, soaking in the adulation. Loving every drop of it.

"Ga-tor! Ga-tor! Ga-tor! Ga-tor!" they start to chant.

As his legally trademarked nickname reverberates through the air, Mark lifts his skateboard triumphantly over his head. GATOR is emblazoned in chunky white lettering across his signature psychedelic-patterned decal board design.

Christian nudges Mark with his elbow. "Check out that bunch of betties," he says. "I think they're into you, man."

He gestures to a cluster of teen girls standing nearby, smiling and waving. They're all wearing cutoff jean shorts and string bikini tops and calling out, "Hi, Gator! Gator, over here! We love you, Gator!"

"Of course they are," Mark scoffs with deliberate, exaggerated bluster. "I'm young. I'm gorgeous. I'm famous. And I'm loaded." Mark waves and blows the girls a kiss. They giggle and blow some back.

Tony rolls his eyes. "Not like it's gone to your head or anything."

But Mark just shrugs him off, and makes a mental note to go talk to those women as soon as he's done skating.

Then he steps onto his board again, angles it over the edge, and hurtles back down the ramp.

CHAPTER 2

Spring 1987

YOU'RE NOT TAKING ME here to kill me...right?"

"Very funny. Just tell me which way to turn, okay?"

In the passenger seat, Brandi McClain, a lithe, seventeen-year-old blond beauty, turns on the dome light and scrutinizes the giant paper map she's unfurled across her lap.

"I think it's a left up at that stop sign," Brandi says. "But are you sure you got the address right, Jess? This neighborhood gives me the creeps."

Brandi's best friend, Jessica Bergsten—also a slim, striking, seventeen-year-old blonde; she could practically pass for Brandi's sister—is behind the wheel of her parents' station wagon. The two girls have been driving for the past ninety minutes, having set out from their homes in a wealthy enclave of Tucson, Arizona, for what Jessica heard from an old friend would be a wild skateboarding party outside Phoenix.

But right now they're cruising through a dark, grim, eerily empty industrial part of the city. Nothing but broken streetlights and abandoned buildings scrawled with graffiti.

"This is the address Christian gave me," Jess answers. "It'll be fine. Just relax."

Brandi tries to distract herself by flipping down the vanity mirror and checking her hair and makeup. She gives her heavily hair-sprayed bangs a quick tease. She reapplies her hot-pink lipstick, the same shade she saw twenty-one-year-old model Cindy Crawford wearing in a recent TV commercial.

A police siren echoes ominously in the distance as Jessica turns left at the stop sign, just as Brandi instructed.

And there it is. At the end of the block stands a massive, multistory warehouse. Rows of high-end cars are parked in front. The sound of punk music rattles from inside.

"Told ya!" Jessica exclaims with a sassy little shimmy. She pulls over to the curb and parks. "Now come on, let's go meet some cute skater boys!"

As the two step into the monstrously cavernous space, Brandi's eyes turn to saucers.

She's attended plenty of high school house parties in her day, but nothing that comes *close* to this. There are flashing, neon-colored lights. A smoke machine. An actual DJ spinning records. A professional bartender pouring cocktails.

And in the center of the warehouse sits a half-pipe that looks cobbled together from pieces of old wood and scrap metal. Skateboarders are clattering up and down the makeshift ramp, catching air and doing all kinds of crazy tricks.

"Jess! You made it!"

A young man with long, flowing black hair rushes up and embraces Jessica, briefly lifting her off her feet.

"Are you kidding? We wouldn't miss it! Christian, this is Brandi."

"Whoa, I didn't know you had a twin!"

Jessica shakes her head. "Please. I *wish* I were as hot as her. We're just friends, but we get that all the time."

"Nice to finally meet you," Brandi says. "Jess said you guys are in town from San Diego for some kind of work event?"

From nowhere, a second skateboarder literally rolls right into their conversation. He abruptly hops off his board and throws an arm around Christian's shoulders.

"Did somebody say *work*? What the heck is that?"

Christian shakes the man off with a flat smile. "He's not kidding."

The mystery skater ignores his friend and focuses instead on Brandi. "I'm Mark," he says. "All my friends call me Gator. But you can call me...anytime you want."

He thrusts his hand at Brandi—who has been left momentarily speechless. She's captivated by this young man's good looks, megawatt smile, and buckets of confidence.

"I'm...uh...I'm Brandi."

"I'm more of a beer and whiskey guy myself, but I can work with that."

Brandi giggles at the joke. Smitten.

Christian says, "This is Jessica. She's a friend of mine from Tucson."

"No way! It's really cool you guys came out tonight," Mark says. "Too bad you missed our skating demo this afternoon. Can I grab you ladies some drinks?"

"I can come with you," Brandi volunteers, just a touch too eagerly.

Mark nods at the offer, pleased. "Right this way."

As they make their way across the crowded party floor, Brandi asks, "So you guys, like, skate for a living?"

"You got it backward. I live to skate. Hopped on my first board when I was seven, haven't stepped off since. All this other stuff? The money, the travel? It's just the cherry on top, you know? Tell me: how long have you been a fan of vert?"

Brandi scrunches her forehead. "A fan of... what?"

Mark laughs. "Ah, I get it. You're more into the *scene* than the sport. The cool clothes. The crazy parties. The whole... stick-it-to-the-man part. Am I right?"

"I guess," Brandi answers with a shrug. But Mark nailed it. Brandi barely knows the difference between a skateboard trick and a card trick. It's the edgy, rebellious allure of skater culture—and skater *boys*—that appeals to something deep inside her.

"Are you still in high school?" Mark asks as they sidle up to the bartending station. "Senior?" Brandi nods. "What do you want to do after you graduate?"

"I want to be a model," she says softly. "That's my dream."

"No shit! You're hot enough for it, that's for sure." Brandi blushes. Mark continues, "Modeling is super fun. I've just started doing some print work myself. Mostly for Vision Street Wear. Heard of them? They're coming out with a whole new line of Gator-branded clothes named after me."

Brandi hesitates. She can't tell if Mark is joking, trying to impress her, or both. "Come on. You seriously have your own clothing line?"

Mark smiles, mysteriously. "Maybe you can... take them off me sometime."

Brandi fully intended to flirt and get some drinks

with Mark and then return to Jessica and Christian. But more and more, she's feeling as though she'd rather spend the rest of the night just talking and laughing and connecting with this cute, unpredictable boy.

His charm, his swagger, his charisma, his boldness—he's like no one she's ever met before in her life.

Brandi finds Mark unbelievably attractive.

And just a little dangerous.

DATING A HUNKY, world-famous skateboarder sure makes it tough to focus on algebra homework.

In the nearly six weeks since Brandi McClain and Mark Rogowski met, she's found it nearly impossible to focus on, well, just about anything besides her dreamy new boyfriend.

Brandi still replays in her mind, again and again, their magical first encounter. She can still feel the tingle of their intense chemistry. Can still smell Mark's enticing musk. Can still recite lines from their wide-ranging conversation, which stretched late into the night and ended with a steamy make-out session at sunrise.

Since then, geographic distance has mostly kept the two young lovers apart. But they've been managing to make their relationship work.

With Brandi living at her parents' home in Tucson and Mark based in San Diego, the pair has kept in touch via phone calls and handwritten letters. By the side of her bed, Brandi keeps a three-ring binder in which she's placed every note Mark has ever mailed to her, each one longer and more emotive than the last, filled with affection and passion and his dreams for their shared future. Discovering that Mark is such a talented wordsmith has been one of the biggest surprises about dating him.

Another surprise is just how wildly successful a pro skateboarder he really is.

The massive fan base. The multiple endorsement deals. Brandi still can't believe the level of fame and fortune twenty-one-year-old Mark has achieved simply by doing tricks in empty swimming pools! She had no idea it was even possible. Mark's career is already very impressive, and as far as she can tell, it's only getting started.

Brandi is halfway through a mind-numbing algebraic problem set when the old rotary phone in her bedroom rings. She leaps up from her desk, shouts "I got it!" to her parents downstairs, and snatches up the handset.

She hears his silky baritone: "Good evening, you sexy thing."

"Mark, stop," Brandi whispers—but secretly, she loves it.

"Whatcha doing? And whatcha wearing?"

Brandi looks down at her open math textbook and then at her ratty T-shirt and grubby sweatpants. Instead of telling the truth, she answers with a titillating tease.

"Oh, nothing much. And…nothing much."

Mark says something in response—but it's drowned out by static.

"Mark? Hello? Are you still there?"

"Sorry, can you hear me now? Maybe we have, like, a bad connection. I'm calling long-distance from Florida."

Did Brandi hear that right? Easing onto her bed, she asks, "Did you say Florida?"

"Yup. We landed this morning! I could've sworn I told you I was coming here in one of my letters, didn't I?"

Brandi doesn't answer. If Mark did mention it, it seems unlikely she'd forget. "Well, anyway, yeah, Bill booked us all for some two-day skate exhibition in Miami. It's amazing down here, babe! The beaches, the booze, the gorgeous w—"

Mark's voice suddenly cuts out again. But this time, there's no static. Brandi is left to wonder if it's the bad connection...or Mark biting his own tongue.

It sure sounded as though he was about to say *gorgeous women*.

She feels her chest tighten at the thought.

Brandi may be only seventeen, but she's not naive. She's well aware that Mark's a young, rich, handsome guy surrounded by fawning, beautiful, half-naked girls everywhere he goes. To Brandi, this makes Mark's apparent devotion to her and their relationship that much more special—and their separation that much harder.

"Mark? I lost you again. What was that last part?"

"Sorry, I was saying the beaches, the booze, and the gorgeous weather down here are all incredible! I wish you were here with me to enjoy it!"

Brandi smiles with relief. "Me, too."

Then Brandi hears some muffled voices on the other end.

"Babe?" Mark says. "I gotta go. We're all grabbing dinner, then going to some press event. Catch ya later!"

"Okay, have fun, miss you, bye!"

Brandi hangs up the phone and leans back against her pillows.

With Mark top of mind, it's going to be extra hard to focus on her math homework now.

But Brandi also knows their situation is temporary. She's in her final semester of high school. And as soon as she graduates, she can move out to California to pursue her dreams of modeling and being with Mark.

Brandi sighs and clutches the binder of letters to her heart—which fully and forever belongs to Gator.

CHAPTER 4

MARK ROGOWSKI LIFTS HIS CHIN. He swivels his hips. He tugs up the hem of the tie-dyed T-shirt he's wearing—a large Vision Street Wear logo is on the front—until it exposes his six-pack abs. He looks directly into the camera. He levels a smoldering gaze.

Bulbs flash. Shutters click.

"Great stuff, Gator! Really hot! Keep it up!"

Mark strikes a few more bad-boy poses as a photographer snaps a flurry of pictures.

Once Mark hears "That's a wrap!" he strides off the indoor set and makes a beeline for the catering table. He's stuffing some sweaty slices of American cheese and a stack of stale Oreos into his mouth when he feels a tap on his shoulder.

"What do you think you're doing?"

Mark turns to see Bill Silva, his slick, smooth-talking manager. A bit paunchy, with curly, shoulder-length brown hair, he's wearing a charcoal blazer and a pair of designer jeans.

"What?" Mark asks, mid swallow. "I'm starving, man!"

"I told you I booked us a table for lunch at Marcelle's."

"So?"

"Gator, Gator, Gator," Bill says, gently taking the cheese and cookies from his star client's hands. "Let me ask you something. Would you ever fill up your Lamborghini with anything less than high-octane premium gasoline?"

Mark gives his manager a sideways look. "Uh, I don't have a Lambo."

Bill smiles. "Wait till I run through the latest numbers with you. You *could*."

Thirty minutes later, the two are tearing into lobsters on the breezy outdoor patio of a high-end bistro in San Diego's upscale Gaslamp District. Most of their fellow diners are businessmen and -women in conservative suits. Mark stands out in his garish T-shirt and board shorts, but instead of feeling self-conscious, he's reveling in the irritated glances and whispers he's getting.

Bill is holding up a magazine and reading aloud from it. "'When I'm skating with my bros, having a good session, fully sweatin' and pumpin' out and rippin', there's like this little volcano inside me that's driving me and heating me. It's better than anything.'" Bill shuts the magazine. "Is that true, Gator? You got a volcano in you when you skate?"

"Hell, yeah. I got a fire in me *all* the time, to be honest. I feel it even more when I'm on my board. But I thought that interview wasn't coming out till the fall."

Bill tosses the magazine across the table. "Hot off the presses. An early copy."

"No way! Rad!"

It's the July 1987 issue of *Thrasher,* a prominent skateboarding magazine with a circulation of a few hundred thousand. On the cover is an action shot of Mark suspended in midair, doing a cool vert trick in an empty swimming pool.

Mark admires the photograph for a moment, and then thumbs to his multipage interview and starts skimming it.

Bill smirks. "I told you I'd make you a cover model, didn't I? But this is just the beginning, Gator. I've got big plans for you and the other guys. Really big."

Mark sets down the magazine, curious. "What kind of plans?"

"First, let's go over where we stand. Your Gator-branded skate decks are flying off the shelves. Skate shops across the country can't restock them fast enough."

"Sweet! I make a buck on every sale, right?"

"*Two* bucks. And we're talking around seven thousand units selling every month. That doesn't include the royalties I negotiated for you on your Gator-branded T-shirts, Gator hats, Gator stickers, Gator fanny packs. Toss in your modeling contracts and endorsement deals? You're doing pretty well for yourself, my friend. Pretty well indeed."

Mark nods and grins. "Of course I am. People freakin' love me!"

Bill takes a sip of sparkling water. "Exactly. And now I want to show advertisers just how *many* people love you. It's your fan base that makes you so special. And so profitable." Bill leans forward in his seat. "So here's what I'm thinking. I want to take you and some of the other extreme athletes I represent on the road. What do you think?"

"You mean, like...do more skate demos and press events?"

"No, no, no. Way bigger. I'm talking, like, touring rock star–level big! I'd put together a whole traveling show. A whole skating *experience*. Lights, music, pyrotechnics—the whole deal. We'd fill arenas all over the country. All over the world!"

Mark has never seen his manager this amped up before. But he's intrigued. *Could I really achieve that level of global fame and celebrity?*

"It would do wonders for your girlfriend's career, too," Bill adds. "Becky, right?"

"Brandi."

"If you got just a few more sponsors backing you? And if she's really as smokin' hot as you keep bragging about—"

"She is, man. Trust me."

"I bet I could start booking you guys some shoots together. As a pair."

"Seriously?"

"Oh, yeah. I can see it now. You'd be one of the hottest couples in the world. Move over, Jagger and Jerry. Here comes Gator and Brandi!"

Mark lets that even wilder notion sink in for a moment. Then he kicks back in his chair and slurps down a meaty chunk of lobster.

"Silva, I freakin' love it. We're in!"

Summer 1987

WHEN THE CAPTAIN ANNOUNCES they're making their initial descent into San Diego, Brandi McClain tightens her grip on her armrests.

Not out of nerves. Out of sheer excitement.

Two weeks ago, Mark Rogowski, her long-distance boyfriend of a couple of months, told her he had bought her a plane ticket to come visit him for the weekend. Since then, she's been counting down the minutes until she gets to see him.

Mark has done this for Brandi a few times before. He's traveled to Arizona twice himself, too. But as Brandi giddily told her best friend, Jessica Bergsten, on the phone last night while she was packing, something about this trip feels...*different* to her. In a good way. She's sure of it, even if she can't quite put her finger on why.

Maybe, Jessica suggested, it's because this may well be the last "visit" to California Brandi ever makes, since she plans to move to San Diego permanently in just a few weeks now that she's graduated high school.

Stepping into the bustling terminal, Brandi feels

her anticipation bubbling up even more. Scanning the crowd for her boyfriend, she takes a few slow, deep breaths to keep herself from trembling.

Mark spots her first and bounds up to her. Before she can say a word, he takes her in his muscular arms and literally sweeps her off her feet.

"Damn, baby, you get more gorgeous every time I see you!"

He sets Brandi down and the two kiss. They are deeply, feverishly in love.

In the airport's short-term-parking garage, Mark casually carries Brandi's luggage past a sparkling white Mercedes-Benz convertible—and then stops, smiles, turns around, and pops the trunk. Brandi is surprised. Mark didn't own this car the last time she visited.

"Nice wheels," she says cheekily. "Bet this thing's a real chick magnet."

Just as cheekily, Mark replies, "I wouldn't know. It's not mine."

He tosses Brandi the keys.

Brandi's smile fades to shock as she realizes what's happening.

"Wait... Hang on... Mark... you don't mean—"

"Think of it as a little congratulations present."

"But... but... congratulations for *what*?"

"I showed Bill that new batch of headshots you sent me. He loves 'em! Says he's already forwarded them to a few local modeling agents he knows and a bunch want to meet with you. You'll be booking jobs in no time."

"No way... Really?!"

"Yep. And I can't have my girlfriend showing up to the set in a rust bucket, can I?"

"Mark, I... I love it. Thank you!"

In an instant, Brandi is back in his arms, their

lips pressed tightly together again. She feels so overwhelmed with joy and gratitude, she nearly breaks down in tears.

"Besides, you'll be moving out here in a couple weeks, right? That's still the plan?"

"Of course!" Brandi exclaims. "Didn't you say you'd help take me to check out some apartments this weekend?"

Mark smiles. "That reminds me. I have another surprise for you."

Speeding up the scenic I-5 freeway with her new convertible's top down and her long blond hair fluttering wildly in the deafening wind, Brandi keeps stealing inquisitive glances at Mark in the passenger seat. He's got his seat reclined and his bare feet resting on the dashboard.

Noticing a sign for Del Mar Heights Road, which she knows is near Mark's place, she yells, "I take exit 34, right?!"

Mischievously, he shakes his head. "Fifty-one B!"

Brandi doesn't know San Diego too well yet, but that sounds awfully far from Mark's apartment. *What could this surprise possibly be?*

Nearly an hour later, she's still following Mark's directions and turns onto a long, winding gravel road. It slices through lush, rolling hills, which are dotted with avocado tree groves that seem to stretch on forever.

With muted awe, Brandi asks, "Where are we?"

"On the map it's called Fallbrook," Mark answers. "But to me, it's heaven."

Finally Brandi pulls into a hidden driveway. At the end is an enormous house unlike any she's seen before. It's tall and narrow, built mostly of wood, with a cylindrical, barrel-shape design.

"Okay, Mark, are you gonna tell me what's going on?"

"Nope. I'm gonna *show* you."

The two exit the convertible and Mark leads Brandi into the house. The inside is even more cavernous than she guessed it would be when she was outside. A central spiral staircase stretches from the ground floor to the top, with various rooms and landings branching off like tree houses connected to the trunk of a mighty oak.

"So?" Mark asks.

"What is this place?"

"My new home! What do you think?"

"You *bought* it? It's amazing! But…it seems like a lot of space for one person."

"Or the perfect amount for *two*. What would you think about moving in together?"

Brandi's chin drops. "Are you serious?!"

"Why not? You could cram into a shoebox with a bunch of random roommates, or you could live in a mansion on a dozen acres with your boyfriend. What do you say?"

Brandi's mouth is still hanging open, but she doesn't make a sound. She can't. The plane ticket, the modeling agents, the new car, and now this?

It's too much! It's almost too good to be true.

"I mean, I should probably ask my parents first," Brandi says ruefully. Then her voice echoes across the empty structure as she yells, "But my answer is yes, yes, yes!"

Within seconds, she and Mark are in each other's arms once again—this time on the bare floor of their future living room, where they are madly shedding their clothes.

CHAPTER 6

BRANDI McCLAIN TWIRLS a springy blond curl around her finger. She runs her tongue seductively across her upper teeth.

"Work it, girl!" says the photographer. "You look stunning! You're a natural!"

It would certainly seem that way.

Since moving to San Diego—and moving in with her boyfriend, Mark Rogowski—a few months ago, Brandi has been booking local modeling jobs left and right. She hasn't broken through onto the national scene yet, but she's well on her way.

The rest of her fairy-tale new life has been falling into place just as smoothly. Mark let her take the lead in furnishing and decorating their quirky Fallbrook house, which she's since turned into a warm and inviting home. And while it took some getting used to after growing up in the suburbs in the Arizona desert, Brandi finds living in such a lush, quiet, rural area to be both peaceful and energizing.

Good thing, too, because she and Mark sure do burn a lot of energy together.

When she first told Jessica that she and Mark would be moving in together, Jessica asked whether Brandi was worried that sharing a roof might dim the couple's flame. Brandi admitted she was.

Fortunately, cohabitating has had the exact opposite effect. After dating long-distance for so many agonizing months, Brandi and Mark can't keep their hands off each other. The love—and lust—they share seems to grow more intense every day.

Finally, after four hours, two wardrobe changes, and three hair and makeup retouches, Brandi's photo shoot wraps for the day and she heads home. Pulling up in her white Mercedes convertible, she sees two cars she recognizes parked in the driveway. They belong to Mark's buddies Christian Hosoi and Tony Hawk.

Sure enough, she finds the three sprawled on the TV room sofa, controllers in hand, playing Nintendo. On the coffee table rests a small mountain of empty beer cans, which might help explain the extra-rowdy atmosphere.

"Dude, watch out for those falling spikes!" Christian cries.

"I see them, idiot!" snaps Tony. "I'm going for the extra power-up!"

"Hi, guys," she calls to her houseguests. "What's up?"

"Hey, baby," Mark hollers back. "How was the shoot?"

"It went great! Thanks for asking. I think they liked me."

"Of course they did," Mark says, smiling at her warmly. "You're gorgeous, you're talented, you're—"

Christian tosses his remote in frustration. "Damn it, Gator, they ate you! Now we gotta start the level over. Pay attention!"

"Chill out, man, would you? My beautiful girlfriend just got home. Think I'd rather look at *her*...or mutant aliens?"

Brandi walks up the spiral staircase and into her and Mark's bedroom.

Their bed is unmade, their sheets still tangled from a wild romp they had that morning. She smiles to herself at the memory.

A few piles of clothing are heaped around the room. Even though their home has lots of closets, Brandi and Mark each receive so much free apparel from their modeling shoots—especially Gator-branded Vision Street Wear—that they simply don't have enough space for it all.

Brandi is in the attached master bathroom, taking off her makeup in the mirror, when she hears the bedroom door creak open.

"Baby?" she says. No answer. "Mark? Is that you?"

Concerned, Brandi reenters the bedroom.

Mark is holding a can of beer, standing in the doorway. Silently. Ominously.

The warmth and good humor he exuded just minutes earlier is completely gone. His face is now etched with dark emotions. Suspicion. Jealousy. Anger.

In a soft but vicious growl he says, "Where the *hell* have you been?!"

The question—and tone—startles Brandi greatly. In the ten months they've been dating, she has never, *ever* seen this side of him, even when he's been drinking.

She responds calmly. "Where have I been? What do you mean? I was working."

"You told me you'd be back by four. It's after five!"

"Okay. Sorry. The shoot ran a little long. Then traffic on the freeway was—"

Mark steps into the bedroom and shuts the door.

Brandi instinctively takes a step back.

"Bullshit!"

The word slices through Brandi like a hot knife.

"Mark…where is this coming from? Why are you so angry? What did I do?"

Mark takes a long, sloppy slug of beer, wipes his mouth with his sleeve.

"That's what I wanna know! If you're living in my house, you're not gonna lie to me! I *always* want to know where you are. Always! Is that clear?!"

Brandi just stands there. Confused. Scared. Desperate to defuse the situation before it gets any worse.

"I…I'm not lying, Mark," she pleads. "I swear. I love you. I would never—"

Mark hurls his half-full beer can across the bedroom. It smashes against the far wall with a metallic crunch.

"Shut up! Just shut up! Shut the f—"

Mark lunges toward Brandi, but suddenly stops himself dead in his tracks.

He stumbles backward a bit. Then looks up at Brandi. And chuckles.

Instantly, he's back to his old, charming self again. As if he's just woken up from some kind of trance.

"Aw, you know I'm only kidding, baby. I just miss you when you're gone!"

Brandi, more unsettled and alarmed than ever, returns a nervous smile.

"Sure. Yeah. I miss you too, Mark."

Mark nods. Then, sheepishly, embarrassed, he opens the bedroom door, shuffles out, and pads back down the spiral staircase.

As soon as he's gone, Brandi shuts and locks the bedroom door, something she's never done before.

She's overcome with relief—as well as a creeping sense of dread.

What in God's name just happened?!

CHAPTER 7

Spring 1989

MARK ROGOWSKI DIDN'T THINK HE had a fear of heights—until now.

He's standing on the narrow platform of a giant half-pipe that's been built mere inches from the edge of a steep cliff in Los Angeles. It's been positioned to perfectly overlook the endless urban sprawl stretching across the San Fernando Valley below.

On a clear day like today, the view is breathtaking—and more than a little nerve-racking. But Mark tries to ignore that and focus on the job at hand.

"Roll camera... and... action!"

On the director's cue, Mark steps onto his skateboard, speeds down the ramp, and begins performing a series of astonishing aerial vert tricks. His girlfriend of the past two years, Brandi McClain, and a handful of other young models and skateboarders all watch and cheer him on.

Out of the corner of Mark's eye, he sees a black convertible with red leather trim slowly pull up in front of the half-pipe. It's driven by a man with shoulder-length blond hair, dark sunglasses, a black cap, and a floral-print jacket.

The other skaters soon join Mark in zooming up and down the ramp. Brandi and the rest of the models continue hooting and hollering even as the man starts singing over a backing track that wafts across the hillside: *"And I'm free...free fallin'! Yeah, I'm free...free fallin'!"*

The singer is Tom Petty. The shoot is part of a music video for a track on Petty's debut solo album. The video is for the song "Free Fallin'," to be released as a single later this year.

"And...cut! Let's take five!"

The skaters stop skating. The models stop cheering. As a production assistant reverses Tom's car back to its starting position, Mark, Brandi, and the others climb down off the ramp. They're immediately swarmed by a team of makeup artists and hair stylists.

"You guys don't have to waste your time working on *this* little lady," Mark says to them, gesturing toward Brandi. "She always looks absolutely perfect."

"Mark, quit it!" Brandi says with a smile, her cheeks turning rosy.

They get even redder when Mark leans over and gives her bottom a firm pat.

It's precisely this smoldering chemistry between Mark and Brandi that has made them one of the skateboarding world's hottest, most in-demand modeling duos—exactly as Mark's manager, Bill Silva, predicted. The two have already appeared together in numerous print ads for Vision Street Wear and more. They've traveled to skating events around the world, in places as far-flung as Brazil and Japan, where they've been cheered by tens of thousands of screaming fans.

Mark and Brandi's fame—and bank accounts—just keeps growing.

"Hey, Gator," calls one of the other skateboarders standing nearby; he's having powder applied to his sweat-dappled forehead. Mark didn't know this guy before they met this morning on set. And after seeing his mediocre skills on the ramp, Mark isn't terribly interested in changing that. In fact, he can't even remember the guy's name.

"Yeah?"

"Can I ask you something? You're one of the kings of vert skating, no question—"

"Damn right I am."

"But what do you think about the rise of street-style skating? Seems to me in the last year or two it's really started getting popular."

Mark scoffs. "Street-style? It'll never catch on. Not in any real way. Trust me."

"I don't know, dude," the skater replies. "A lotta kids seem to be getting into it."

"It's just a lame fad. It's lazy. It's boring. In vert, you do all kinds of fun, crazy shit. Like shifties and frogstands, ollies and gazelle flips, up and down ten-foot ramps. In street-style, all you do is grind on park benches and sidewalk curbs for a few seconds. *Snore*."

"But isn't that, like, the whole point?" Brandi interjects. "You don't need a half-pipe or an empty swimming pool to skate. Anybody can do it, anywhere. I love that!"

Mark glares at Brandi and shakes his head, to the irritation of his makeup artist.

"*Do* it, maybe. But *watch* it? Actually give a shit about it? Last I checked, anybody, anywhere, can play basketball with a broken milk crate tied to a telephone pole. Do you think millions of NBA fans are going to start paying attention? Gimme a break."

Mark is certain that vert skating is here to stay—and that it's only going to get bigger. He's also supremely confident that he's going to remain a top skater for many, many years to come. After all, he's already a minor global celebrity at age twenty-three, with more money than he knows what to do with. Not to mention he's got Brandi, the hottest woman he's ever met. He's living a charmed life, and he fully expects it to stay that way.

"Places, everybody! We're about to go again!"

Mark, Brandi, and the others climb back up onto the half-pipe ledge and get ready for the next take. Mark looks over at his girlfriend and gives her a quick, sexy wink.

But then he makes the mistake of glancing down over the cliff's edge.

It's a long, long way to the bottom.

CHAPTER 8

SPINNING HEELFLIP TO A FRONTSIDE *disco spin. Five-forty into an ollie airwalk.*

His eyes squeezed shut, Mark Rogowski is visualizing his next run of tricks, up and down the ramps he knows so well here at his beloved Del Mar Skate Ranch. This is the place where vert skating—and his career—first began, just a few short years ago.

Mark takes a deep breath and then opens his eyes.

And slumps with despair.

Mark isn't perched on a ramp. He's standing outside the park's main gate, which is secured tightly with rusty chains and a padlock the size of a bowling ball.

Some time ago, the owners of Del Mar Skate Ranch abruptly shut down the park, after selling the property to a hotel developer. Jackhammers quickly reduced its warren of concrete jumps and half-pipes to pits of rubble. Gone, too, are the hordes of fans. And instead of the pleasant scent of the Pacific, the air reeks of diesel fuel and tar.

Mark gives the gate's metal bars a forlorn, futile

shake. He considers hopping the fence, just to wander around the former grounds, despite a large sign that reads NO TRESPASSING, VIOLATORS WILL BE PROSECUTED. A mischievous vandalizer has spray-painted over some words to make it read NO ASS VIOLATORS.

Mark snickers at the childish joke.

But inside, his heart is breaking.

This isn't the first time he's paid a visit to the shuttered Del Mar park since its untimely demise. But it will probably be his last. The memories this place brings back are just too painful. Memories of happier times. Of easier times.

Of more successful times.

About a half hour later, Mark pulls up behind Brandi's white convertible, parked in their driveway.

Their *new* driveway.

Recently, the pair moved from the house in rural Fallbrook to a comfortable but much more modest two-bedroom condo in the coastal town of Carlsbad. It was partly because Brandi had grown tired of living out in the boonies, so far from work and friends, the ocean and the city.

But mostly, even if Mark refuses to admit it, it was because the once highly paid skateboarding star simply could no longer afford the mansion.

Mark trudges inside and makes a beeline for the cramped kitchen. Swiping a bottle of beer from the fridge, he chugs it, draining it in seconds. As he cracks open a second, Brandi enters. "Hey," she says brightly. "Good: you're home."

"If you can call this dump that," Mark huffs.

Brandi ignores the snide comment. "Bill called three times today. He's really been trying to get ahold of you. Says it's important."

Mark scoffs at the idea that Bill Silva, his longtime

manager, could have anything noteworthy to say. "How damn important could it be? Bill hasn't booked me anything in forever."

"Which is exactly why you should phone him back. It could be good news!"

Begrudgingly, Mark does so.

"Gator!" exclaims Bill, his tone chipper and upbeat. "How's it hangin'?"

Mark wants to answer with the truth: *by a goddamn thread*. But the enthusiasm in his manager's voice gives him pause—and a tiny glimmer of hope.

"I'm doing all right, man. Yeah, thanks. So what's up?"

Bill lets out a slow stream of air.

"So...listen. I know these last few months—the last year, really—haven't been great for us. I wish I could tell you that's going to change. Instead I'm calling because...well, I've been hearing a rumor. A not-so-great one. Thought you deserved to know."

"What rumor? Spit it out."

"Vision's profits are way down. There's talk about a possible bankruptcy. Which means I think they're going to want to renegotiate your contract."

Mark feels his breath catch in his throat. He's been under a lucrative modeling and product sponsorship deal with Vision Street Wear for years. Especially now, it makes up a huge chunk of his income.

"Shut up. Are you serious?! I'm their number one seller!"

"You *used* to be. Truth is, your branded skate decks, your T-shirts...Gator merchandise just isn't moving like it once did. Look, we gotta face the facts here. Kids are losing interest in vert skating. Now it's all about the *next* generation: street-style skaters."

Mark is shattered by what he's hearing.

"The next generation?! I'm twenty-three! And street skating sucks. It's a total joke!"

"Hey, I know that. You know that. But the marketing bigwigs are convinced—"

"Well, screw them! And screw you, too!"

Mark slams down the phone. In a haze of fury and desperation, he gulps down the rest of the beer he's holding and then storms out of his condo, grabbing one of the skateboards propped up by the front door.

"Street skating?!" Mark grumbles angrily to himself, marching onto his driveway. "Pathetic little ollies off a sidewalk? Dinky little kickflips in the middle of a flat street? If that's the shit you people want to see...fine! How hard could it be?"

Mark drops his board and starts to ride. When he reaches the curb, he tries to sail off—but he times the jump wrong and nearly loses his balance.

"Damn it!"

Mark recovers and keeps skating, making wide figure eights around his quiet cul-de-sac. He tries to jump and get some air with his board, but without the help of a ramp, he can't do it. He tries again but loses his footing and just barely rights himself.

Growing frustrated, Mark tries one more time. He crouches extra low, leaps extra high—but he stumbles and face-plants on the concrete. Hard.

"Shit, man, I suck!"

Painfully, Mark picks himself up. Then he grabs his board—and smashes it against the street. Again and again, until the GATOR-logoed wood cracks and splinters.

Mark finally stops. Catches his breath. Suddenly self-conscious about what he's done, he slowly turns back to face his home.

Brandi is standing at the window, watching him, arms crossed in concern.

CHAPTER 9

Late 1989

OF ALL THE THOUSANDS of people swimming, sunbathing, and otherwise enjoying this picture-perfect day at San Diego's Mission Beach, only one person is wearing a colorfully embroidered bolero jacket and a pair of rawhide cowboy boots.

Augie Constantino leans back against the boardwalk's railing. Resting the heel of his boot on a skateboard, he surveys the crowd.

Still no sign of him.

Augie checks his watch. Strokes his bushy goatee. Then he pulls out the business card tucked in the pocket of his stonewashed jeans pocket and reads it for the hundredth time: MARK "GATOR" ROGOWSKI, SKATEBOARDER EXTRAORDINAIRE.

Augie smiles, recalling the divine intervention that led him to this exciting moment.

A few days ago, while out surfing, Augie's wife struck up a conversation with a nice young man walking along the beach. He turned out to be a famous skateboarder and gave her his card. Sensing that God had brought this Gator guy into their lives for a reason,

Augie gave him a call. On the phone, Mark seemed distant. Dispirited. Very much in need of guidance and salvation. Augie suggested the two meet up. Mark didn't seem very interested—until Augie revealed that he, too, was a skateboarder and had a promising business opportunity he wanted to share.

Augie looks up. Despite the droves of gangly, long-haired dudes ambling along the boardwalk carrying skateboards, Augie has a special feeling about this one.

He calls out, "Excuse me. Are you Mark?"

"Yeah. Hey. You must be Augie?" As the two shake hands, Mark eyes Augie's leather boots. "Don't tell me you actually skate in those things?"

"Sure I do. The Lord protects my life, but these protect my feet."

Mark shrugs. "Uh...okay."

At Augie's suggestion, the two turn and start strolling together down the boardwalk.

"I have a confession to make," Augie tells Gator. "I'm a little starstruck right now. You probably get that all the time. You're an absolute legend in the skating world."

Mark averts his eyes. "I guess so. Thanks. You said you skate, too?"

"All the time. I actually started off as a pro surfer. I was living in Hawaii. One night, I had a few too many. Got behind the wheel...*bam*. Next thing I know, I'm lying in the hospital." Augie gestures to his thigh and then to his right eye, which has a slightly limp lid. "I severed my quadriceps. Nearly lost my vision. I knew my surfing career was over."

Mark nods pensively. "So you couldn't surf anymore, but you could skate?"

"Skateboarding is simply a tool I use. To connect with people."

"Uh...I'm not really following you, man. And what does this have to do with *me*?"

"On the night of my accident, I believe God was watching over me. He saved my life. So I devoted it to Him. I dedicated myself to spreading the word of Jesus Christ."

Mark stops walking and turns to Augie, disappointed.

"Dude, come on. You said you had a business thing you wanted to talk about. I need money. If I knew you were just some religious nut, I never would have—"

"Hang on, I do have a business proposition. Hear me out. I work for a wonderful place not far from here called Calvary Chapel. I'm what I like to call a skateboard minister. I use the sport as a way to reach young people and share with them the teachings of the Lord. If someone as famous and influential in the skating world as *you* were to join us, I know we could have an even bigger impact on—"

Mark throws up his hands in annoyance.

"Enough. I get it. No thanks. I don't mean to be rude, but that ain't my thing."

Augie offers a kind smile. "I understand. But my door is always open if you change your mind. Or...if you're ever feeling lost, Mark. Confused. Alone. Unsure of the right path to take in your life. God will tell you the answer. All you have to do is listen."

Mark bites his lip. Absorbs Augie's words for a moment. It seems they might have struck a chord. Then Mark drops his board and hops on. "Nah. I'm good. Catch ya 'round."

Augie watches him skate off.

But something tells him he'll be seeing Gator again.

CHAPTER 10

Summer 1990

HALLO UND WILLKOMMEN to the Hotel Schön, gentlemen. Please enjoy your stay."

Keys in hand, Mark Rogowski and the gaggle of other pro skaters he's traveling with all pile into the elevator and race to their rooms.

This team, sponsored by Vision, is in West Germany for a weeklong vert skateboarding tournament. The style might be losing popularity in the U.S., but it still has a decent following here in Europe. At least for now.

Mark sets down his bags. "Incoming!" he hollers, and belly flops onto the king-size bed. He hears the bed frame snap, which makes him howl with laughter.

Flipping over, he gazes out his hotel window. The whole team is staying on this floor, which looks out over a bustling city street. The sun is just starting to set. Down the block is a construction site, ringed with fencing. A crane is lifting a piece of rebar high into position. Mark watches. Something about it is mesmerizing. Almost hypnotic.

His room phone rings. "Guten Tag, sexy," he answers, expecting it to be Brandi.

"Gross, Gator. Keep it in your pants."

It's actually John Hogan, the traveling team's manager. He's not only a fellow skater but also in charge of keeping an eye on his young, reckless teammates—even though he's pretty much the same age.

"Where are you, dude?" John asks. "We're all in the lobby. We're going out!"

Within minutes, they're at the closest neighborhood bar the group can find, and it's Mark's turn to pay for a round of Jägermeister shots.

This isn't the team's first drink that night. And it definitely isn't their last.

"Here's to the greatest damn vert skate team in the world!" Mark declares, hoisting his dark-hued drink high into the air. John and the others do the same.

They cheer. They clink. They drink.

They repeat. Again. And again. They go to a second bar. Then a third.

Hours later, now well into the night, Mark stumbles out of the men's room. His head is spinning. His legs are wobbling. But he's having a grand time.

He manages to make it back to the busy bar area, but to his surprise, John and the rest of his team are gone. The gang was planning to go to one last spot, but Mark assumed they'd wait for him to get out of the john.

"Dumb assholes," he mumbles, more amused than annoyed.

Mark steps outside. Still no sign of them.

With a sigh, he decides his best bet is to head back to the hotel and wait. But where the hell is it? Looking up and down the dark, foreign, unfamiliar German street, Mark struggles to get his bearings.

Then he sees something peeking over the buildings.

The construction crane he glimpsed earlier from his window.

He heads toward it. It's only a few blocks away. But with each clumsy step he takes, Mark feels himself getting drunker and drunker. The Jägermeister is hitting him hard. Every few feet, he has to cling to a streetlamp to keep himself upright. He leans over and throws up into a gutter. Twice.

Mark finally reaches the edge of the now-vacant construction site. He grasps on to the spiked, wrought-iron fencing for support. He looks around for the hotel.

Shit, which way is it now? Left? Right?

He knows it's here somewhere. If only he could get a better view.

Like from a higher vantage point.

His foolish, drunken idea taking shape, Mark homes in on the towering metal crane.

John Hogan wakes up to a frantic knocking on his hotel-room door.

It's after three in the morning. Still wearing his clothes and sneakers from earlier that night, he's lying passed out on top of his bed, facedown, having collapsed almost the second he staggered in.

John tries to ignore the knocking—until he hears "Hogan?! It's Gator! Open up!"

John grunts. Rubs his eyes. He's irritated at being roused but relieved that Mark made it back to the hotel after somehow getting separated from the rest of the group a few hours ago. When they went back to look for him, he was gone. John was concerned, but not terribly. He knew Gator was tough. He'd be just fine.

John drags himself out of bed. Shuffles over to open the door.

"Holy shit!" he exclaims, nearly tripping backward in shock.

Mark is drenched in blood. Thick and syrupy, flowing literally from head to toe.

He has a massive gash on the side of his face and numerous gaping puncture wounds on his hands and forearms. All wounds are bleeding profusely, with the speed and sound of soda pouring out of a can.

Mark looks woozy. Dazed. He's standing upright but seems barely conscious.

"What the hell happened to you, man?! I need to get your ass to a hospital!"

"I'm...I..." Mark wheezes, badly slurring his words. "I...think I fell."

"Jesus Christ! Fell from *where*?! How?!"

Mark smiles, his teeth drenched with blood. "I dunno. Guess I thought I could fly."

Hitching a ride in the back of the speeding ambulance, John watches in stunned silence as a team of German paramedics work quickly to bandage and stabilize his teammate and friend.

Mark, on the other hand, is flailing around wildly, screaming gibberish at the top of his lungs like a madman.

It's obvious he's in utter agony from his injuries. The booze and endorphins must be wearing off, and the pain meds haven't yet kicked in.

Still, thrashing and shrieking, Mark looks like a tweaker strung out on PCP.

"You're gonna be okay, Gator!" John calls out. "Hang in there, buddy! They'll have you stitched up and back to your old self in no time!"

But deep down, John knows there's no way that's true.

Whatever happened to Mark, it's a damn miracle he's even still alive.

CHAPTER 11

Fall 1990

FOR THE KINGDOM, THE POWER, and the glory are yours, now and forever. Amen."

A chorus of voices repeats "Amen."

Sitting on a metal folding chair, Mark Rogowski lifts his bowed head and flutters open his eyes. His expression is one of total peace and serenity.

Seated beside him, Augie Constantino smiles and rests a hand on Mark's shoulder. "Thank you, Mark. That was lovely." Then he turns to the rest of this intimate, nine-person prayer circle. "Now let's all get out there and have a blessed and joyful day!"

Mark, Augie, and the other participants file out of Calvary Chapel. In the parking lot, the group exchanges hugs and good-byes under the warm morning sun.

Mark gets into Augie's car with him. "I was thinking," he says, "maybe we could hang out on Scripps Pier today. It's the start of fall break at UCSD. La Jolla's beaches are gonna be packed. Just think of all the students we could talk to, all in one place."

Augie practically shines with pride. "Mark, that's an inspired idea!"

Later that morning, Mark and Augie take up positions on opposite ends of the boardwalk. Augie is on cowboy-booted foot, but Mark is on his skateboard. With a Bible quite literally in hand, he's riding slowly up and down the pier, trying to strike up a conversation with anyone who will listen.

He's not having much luck.

But then Mark notices a trio of teenage boys strolling along, one of whom is holding a skateboard of his own. Seeing his way in, Mark rides over to intercept them.

"Hey, guys, what's up? Got a couple minutes to hear about the Lord?"

"Sorry, dude," one of them says. "Not interested."

Another adds, "Yeah, don't waste your time with us anyway. We're huge sinners—and proud of it!"

The group laughs. Mark doesn't.

"Hey, I get it. I used to be that way, too. Until I saw the light. Now I—"

"Shit, hold up," says the third young man, the one holding the skateboard. He looks at Mark with surprised recognition. "I know you…You're Gator Rogowski!"

Mark politely shakes his head.

"No, I'm not. My name is Mark Anthony."

"Huh? Dude, I had a poster of you up in my bedroom when I was a kid! Used to watch you skate at Del Mar all the time. You're the man! You're Gator freaking Rog—"

"I'm *not,*" Mark answers, more firmly this time. "Not anymore. Gator was my name before I was saved. And Rogowski was the name of my father—who abandoned me and my mother when I was three. Now I have a new father. A heavenly one."

The teen makes a face. "Damn, Gator. What the hell

happened to you? You used to be a total badass. Now you're, like, selling Bibles?"

"I'll tell you what happened," Mark replies. "A few months ago, I was on tour. I had a terrible accident. I almost died. I *should* have died. But I didn't. I believe Jesus Christ spoke to me through that accident. I used to be a blind dude, but now I can see. And I'm not selling a thing. God's love is infinite and all around us, and completely free."

The three teens trade snarky, skeptical looks.

"Whatever, man. You want to be some Jesus freak now? Cool. Not us."

The trio moves on, whispering and cackling.

Mark is disappointed but undeterred. He continues his skateboard evangelizing for a few more hours until he and Augie break for lunch: boardwalk hot dogs and ice-cold sodas.

"So how's it been going on your end?" Augie asks, squirting a packet of mustard on his dog.

"About the same as always," Mark answers. "It's tough to talk about God to people who aren't ready to listen. But I think I'm getting better."

"That's awesome! Every soul you connect with matters. Even if it's just one. And even if you're just planting the seed. Eventually, that seed will grow."

Mark nods. He knows he's living proof.

After he came home to San Diego a few months ago following his near-death ordeal in West Germany, Mark suddenly began to feel a strange but powerful spiritual calling, one he'd never felt before. He reached back out to Augie, who rushed to his bedside, and stayed there for every step of his physical recovery and religious rebirth. Since then, the two have become nearly inseparable friends—and recently colleagues, too.

"Thanks, man," Mark replies. "I know *you* know

the work that we're doing is important. I just wish the *other* people in my life understood that. Like, last night in bed, I was trying to talk to Brandi about it, but she kept—"

"Whoa, whoa, whoa," Augie says, holding up a palm. "What bed?"

Mark groans. "Man, come on. Don't start with that right now, okay?"

"Mark, why is this so hard for you to understand? Of course Brandi isn't going to fully understand the spiritual journey you're on. We're all sinners, but you two are actively choosing to *live in sin*...together! Either marry her or move out and stay celibate until you do—and until she sees the light. You can't have it both ways."

Mark hangs his head. He's deeply torn.

What are they going to do?

CHAPTER 12

WHAT DO YOU MEAN, *What are we going to do?*" asks Brandi.

She's in the kitchen, chopping lettuce, making a simple salad for dinner.

Mark has just arrived home after another long day spent wandering up and down the boardwalk, pestering strangers, rambling about Jesus.

He already has a beer in his hand.

It's already almost empty.

"I mean, I've been thinking," he says, "and we gotta make some changes around here, babe. This isn't the way God wants us to live. It isn't the way *I* want us to live."

Brandi was in a fine mood just moments ago. Now she's feeling tense. She has her guard up, bracing for a fight with her newly born-again boyfriend.

Mark's extreme religious beliefs are starting to take a real toll on their relationship. It's driving a wedge between them. And it's only getting worse. It's been a few months since Mark's drunken accident in West

Germany sparked this sudden, fanatical interest in Christianity, and Brandi is still getting used to it.

Truth be told, she still isn't sure she buys it. Not completely. Nor do plenty of mutual friends she's talked to about it. Brandi has often wished she could confide in Jessica, her onetime best friend back in Arizona, but the two have lost touch.

Part of Brandi suspects that Mark's religious awakening is all an act. A gimmick. A last-ditch marketing effort to reinvent himself and revive his floundering skating career.

Or maybe she just hopes that's what this is. Because her boyfriend sure hasn't been making much money lately. Not from skateboarding, not from modeling, not from anything else.

"What *kind* of changes do you want us to make?" Brandi asks warily.

"Well, for starters," Mark says, "I still wish you'd convert. Or at least seriously think about it some more. Maybe you'll reconsider."

Brandi stiffens. "Mark, we've talked about this. You can pray and worship however you want. That's fine by me. Really. But I am *not* converting to some religion I don't believe in. It's not gonna happen."

"Baby, I used to feel that way, too. I was—"

"Blind and now you can see," Brandi snaps. "Yeah. I know. You've only told me that a hundred times."

With a grimace, Mark twists open another bottle of beer.

"Okay, fine. But if you're not gonna get baptized, you have to at least start coming to church more with me and Augie."

To Brandi's credit, she did try going to Mark's new church, Calvary Chapel, a few times, but it wasn't her thing at all. Too boring. Too preachy. Too creepy.

But that's not why Mark's comment gets under her skin.

"I *have* to go to church, do I? I don't *have* to do anything, thank you very much."

Mark's nostrils flare in anger. "You're wrong. We *all* have to follow the words and teachings of Jesus Christ, Brandi. At least those of us who don't want to end up in hell."

Brandi sets down her knife and spins to face her boyfriend.

"Are you even hearing yourself, Mark? You sound nuts! And for someone so worried about going to hell all of a sudden, you sure do drink a lot—and have plenty of premarital sex!"

Mark takes a long pull of his beer.

"That's another thing we gotta change. We can't do that anymore. Not until we're married. In fact, you can't keep living with me, either. Not until you're my wife."

Brandi throws back her head and laughs. What Mark just said is beyond absurd.

"You're joking, right? Now, after years of screwing our brains out, you're telling me we have to stop—*and* you're kicking me out?! You're gonna toss me out onto the street?! That sure doesn't sound very Christian to me!"

Mark's eyes narrow. His voice rises. "You don't know the first thing about being a good Christian!"

"And you do? Hanging out with that weirdo all day makes you an expert?"

"Watch it," Mark warns. "Augie's my spiritual adviser. He's my friend. And he's brilliant!"

"Gimme a break! He's a washed-up loser, with nothing else going for him in his life except his stupid religion...just like you!"

Mark turns away from Brandi, visibly hurt.

He simmers silently for a few seconds.

Then he turns back.

And without warning, he lunges at her.

Brandi shrieks with terror as Mark shoves her out of the kitchen and drags her down the hallway.

"Mark, what the hell? Stop! You're hurting me!"

Blinded by rage, Mark ignores her pleas.

He flings open the door of the coat closet. It's stuffed with clothes and old skateboarding gear. There's barely any room inside.

"Now get in there and keep quiet!"

"Mark, what are you—"

But Brandi is powerless to resist as Mark hurls her into the closet and slams the door.

Inside, it's instantly, terrifyingly pitch-dark.

Brandi hears Mark scrape a piece of furniture along the floor outside the closet. Then she hears him storm out of the condo.

Brandi crumples to the ground in a heap of sobs. She has never, *ever* seen that side of her boyfriend before.

And it scares her to death.

After a few moments, Brandi pulls herself together. Satisfied that Mark isn't coming back, she tries to push open the closet door.

But she can't.

She tries again.

It won't budge.

Finally, with a great deal of effort—because Mark seems to have hastily dragged an easy chair in front of the closet door to keep Brandi "locked" inside—she manages to get the door open a few inches. Pushing with all her strength, she is able to slip out.

Brandi catches her breath. Wipes her eyes. And makes a plan.

Mark says he wants her out of their house?

Fine. He'll get his wish.

Brandi decides she's leaving that night—and never coming back.

CHAPTER 13

Six weeks later

THIS LASAGNA'S DELICIOUS, Mrs. McClain. Thanks again for having me over for dinner. It's totally rad getting to meet you guys!"

"You're very welcome. We're glad you're here. Brandi's told us both so much about you."

Brandi smiles and nods in agreement and then reaches over and tenderly touches her new boyfriend's arm.

It's been about six weeks since Mark blew a gasket and locked her in a closet. It took less than half an hour for Brandi to gather up all her clothes and belongings, pile them into her white Mercedes convertible, and hit the road before he came home—which was both the easiest and the hardest decision she's ever had to make.

Brandi loved Mark deeply. Over the three years they were together, she was by his side, through his professional highs and lows. And she felt she did her very best to be patient with his career struggles and supportive of his religious awakening. But she wasn't ever going to convert to Evangelicalism. She wasn't going to start going to church. She wasn't going to get married anytime soon, or give up having sex.

And she *definitely* wasn't going to put up with any physical abuse.

But with her nascent modeling career and her new friends all in Southern California, Brandi wasn't about to move back to Arizona.

Luckily, she didn't have to. Brandi's mother and stepfather recently relocated from Tucson to Canyon Lake, a quiet, gated community about halfway between San Diego and LA. After crashing on a friend's couch the first night she fled Mark's condo, Brandi made the hour drive north and moved in with her folks.

Brandi also started casually dating a new guy.

Blond, blue-eyed, built like a Viking, he's supremely chill and laid-back. And he doesn't give a hoot about religion. The only commandment he seems to follow is, "Thou shalt have as much hot sex as possible."

"Brandi tells us you're a professional surfer?" her stepfather asks.

"Yeah! I've been catching waves since forever, but I didn't turn pro until I was—"

Suddenly, the phone rings.

And all four people at the dinner table freeze.

Brandi's stepfather starts to push back his chair. "Excuse me. Let me get that."

"No," Brandi replies sternly. "Don't. It could be *him*. It probably is. I just know it."

Her stepfather frowns, frustrated, but obeys as the phone keeps ringing.

At last the answering machine picks up. After the beep, Brandi, her new boyfriend, her mother, and her stepfather all collectively hold their breath.

A man's voice growls, *"Pick up the damn phone, you bitch! I know you're there!"*

The voice belongs to Mark Rogowski—who hasn't been taking their breakup well at all.

For the past few weeks, he's been showing up at the clothing boutique where Brandi has been working part-time. He's started following her and her new boyfriend around town. Increasingly jealous and obsessive, he's been accosting them. *Threatening* them.

Most recently, Mark somehow learned Brandi's mother and stepfather's home phone number. He's started leaving long, angry, deeply disturbing messages at all hours of the day and night.

"You can't keep ignoring me forever, you dumb bitch! You think you know what I'm capable of? You have no idea, Brandi, no idea at all! You're gonna fry in hell!"

Mark slams the phone down, and the answering machine goes silent.

"That's it," Brandi's mother announces. "We're calling the police."

Dabbing her moist eyes, Brandi replies, "Mom, no. I don't want to."

Brandi's stepfather interjects, "Honey, we *have* to. Mark's behavior is getting worse. His messages are getting scary."

Brandi knows her parents are right. But somewhere inside her, she also feels a lingering sympathy toward her former longtime boyfriend. She wants him to stop bothering her, but she doesn't want to ruin his life.

"I know," Brandi answers. "It's just...Let's give him a little more time, okay? He's upset. They're just words. He's just blowing off steam. I'm sure he'll cut it out soon."

"How can you be sure?" her mother asks. "You just

heard what that boy said, honey. We have no idea what he's capable of!"

Brandi chews on her mother's ominous words.

She's scared and hates to admit it.

But her mother is absolutely right.

CHAPTER 14

PEDALING HER BICYCLE ALONG a quiet, tree-lined road through the foothills of Canyon Lake—she's heading home after a daytime shift at the boutique—Brandi inhales deeply. The pleasing scent of freshly fallen leaves hangs in the crisp, clean air.

Around the corner is the main entrance to the private community where she continues to live with her mother and stepfather.

Brandi brakes as she arrives at the gatehouse. It's about the size of a large toolshed, with a mission-style red-tile roof. A middle-aged man wearing a navy-blue uniform and sporting a bushy mustache steps up to the window.

"Hi, Lou," calls Brandi with a friendly wave.

"Evening, Miss McClain," answers the security guard. "Welcome home."

A moment later, the retractable metal arm lifts and Brandi continues riding down the private road.

She's been living here for a good two months now and has gotten to know most of the guards well enough that they no longer ask her for ID every time she enters. Was it a small nuisance at first? For sure. But Brandi was, and continues to be, extremely grateful for the extra security—especially given her ex-boyfriend Mark's recent behavior.

Which, thankfully, appears to be in the past.

Mark hasn't shown up at her work or left any threatening phone messages on her home machine in nearly two weeks. Just as Brandi hoped, it seems as though they're both finally moving on with their lives, no police intervention necessary.

Brandi hops off her bike in front of her mother and stepfather's house, leaving it propped up right there in the driveway. That's another perk of living in a gated community: the chances of being burglarized are very, very…

"What the—?"

Stepping up to the front door, Brandi sees that it's slightly ajar.

Neither of her parents should be home from work yet, and neither of their cars is in the driveway. Did one of them accidentally leave the door open in the rush to leave this morning?

Or is there another explanation?

Could somebody else have left it open—or broken in?

Could that person be inside the house right now?

Brandi's mind immediately leaps to Mark—but just as quickly, she shoves that thought aside. His car isn't in the driveway, and she doesn't see it parked on her block. And besides, he couldn't have gotten past the guardhouse even if he wanted to. Brandi's mother and stepfather have explicitly warned security about Mark and his behavior, and have asked the guards to keep an eye out. No way they would ever let him pass.

Right?

Steeling her nerves, Brandi pushes open the front door and enters.

The house is dark and quiet. But nothing looks out of place.

"Hello?" she calls out. "Anybody here?"

Brandi waits. Listens. For a voice. For footsteps. For any sound at all.

She hears nothing.

Exhaling with relief and feeling just a little silly, Brandi heads upstairs to her bedroom. She flips on the lights.

And gasps.

The room has been completely ransacked, from wall to wall.

Her closet has been thrown open, her wardrobe left in total disarray.

Her dresser drawers have been overturned, their contents spilled everywhere.

For a few seconds, Brandi is too shocked and overwhelmed to speak.

Silently, carefully, she surveys the damage.

She notices something odd.

Numerous pieces of designer clothing, along with much of her jewelry, are missing. But a lot has been left behind. What kind of burglar, she wonders, would walk off with *some* expensive items but not others?

Then Brandi notices something else, and pieces the puzzle together.

Strewn across the carpet is a collection of glass picture frames she's been keeping in a box in the back of her closet. Most of the frames contain old photographs of herself, her family, and her friends.

One—and only one—glass frame has been smashed, the photo inside ripped out and torn to shreds.

It was a picture of Brandi lying on a patch of grass, curled up happily next to Mark.

Feeling equal parts violated and furious, Brandi grabs the cordless phone in her room and dials 911. She's livid yet manages to calmly explain to the operator what she believes happened: her ex-boyfriend must have somehow charmed his way past security, trespassed onto private property, broken into her family's home, and stolen every piece of clothing and jewelry he ever bought for her. Her ex-boyfriend has shown himself to be not only dangerous and unbalanced but spiteful and petty.

Phone still in hand, Brandi heads downstairs and back outside to wait for the cops—where she makes one final, unnerving discovery.

Noticing that the garage door has also been left ajar, she opens it fully.

Her white Mercedes convertible—another gift from Mark—is missing.

All Brandi can do at this point is laugh.

But perhaps there's a silver lining in all of this. Having taken back everything he ever gave her, Mark has no reason to bother Brandi anymore. Maybe he'll finally leave her alone, once and for all.

At least that's what she hopes.

CHAPTER 15

SPREADING THE GOOD WORD ALL DAY can really work up an appetite.

Mark Rogowski and Augie Constantino have been *witnessing,* as they call it—pacing and skateboarding up and down busy Coronado Beach, stopping and proselytizing to as many people as they can—since about nine o'clock this morning. They got so caught up in it that their "lunch" was a bag of chips and a couple of candy bars, scarfed down in about five minutes.

Now it's nearly seven, and the two young evangelicals are starving. They each grab a slice of pepperoni pizza from the boardwalk and plop down on the curb out front.

"Gosh, I'm beat," Augie declares, "but I feel fantastic! I think I really connected with a lot of folks out there today. What about you, man?"

Mark doesn't respond. Instead he's staring down at his greasy slice, his mind somewhere far away. He pinches the bridge of his nose.

Then he lets out a muffled sob.

Which catches Augie completely by surprise. "Whoa! What's wrong, brother?"

"I…I just miss her so much," Mark answers, his voice cracking. "Brandi. I've been thinking about her all day. I can't stop! I still love her…but I hate her! And I hate myself for…"

"Hey, come on, now," Augie says, scooting closer to his dear friend and tossing an arm around his shoulders. "Don't talk like that. With Jesus in your heart, there's no room for hate of any kind. Not toward anyone. Least of all yourself."

Mark shakes his head. "You don't know what I've been saying and doing to her, Augie. The things I've been *thinking* about saying and doing to her."

Augie hesitates, as if nervous to ask. "Mark? You haven't…hurt her, have you?"

"No! Of course not! And I"—Mark's voice softens as he finishes the sentence—"I never would. Just stupid shit. Like following her and her new boyfriend around. Leaving weird messages on her machine. A couple weeks ago? I even snuck into—I mean, uh…I made her give me back a bunch of gifts and shit I'd given her."

Uncomfortable, Mark looks at the ground. "There's something else, too," he continues. "It's kind of embarrassing."

Augie waits to hear it, completely nonjudgmental.

"I don't just miss Brandi's soul," Mark says. "I miss…her *body*. You know what I'm saying? The flesh is weak, dude. I've got needs. And lately, I've been turning to some pretty sinful movies and magazines to satisfy them. I wish I could quit. I know I should. But sometimes it feels like it's out of my control."

Mark braces for the tongue-lashing he expects Augie to unleash on him. After all, what could be more wicked and shameful than having an addiction to pornography?

Instead all Augie gives his friend is love.

"I hear you, man. Can I come clean about something, too? I used to wrestle with that same filthy demon myself."

"You? No way. Really?"

"Oh, sure. The power of porn is very real. I struggled with it for quite a while before I finally kicked the habit for good."

"How'd you do it?"

Augie pulls out and holds up the pocket-size red-leather Bible he keeps with him at all times.

"Galatians 6:1: 'Keep watch on yourself, lest you too be tempted.' To me, that means removing temptation in the first place. One day, I tossed out my entire porno stash and made a promise to God to never buy any more ever again."

"You don't think I've tried that?" Mark huffs. "It's not that easy, dude."

"Of course it isn't. But you've got to start somewhere. Hey, why don't I come over right now and help you rid your home of that smut once and for all?"

Mark considers the offer but balks.

"I appreciate that, man. But…nah, not tonight. Another time. I promise."

"Okay," Augie answers. "Whenever you're ready, let me know. I'll be there."

Mark takes a hearty bite of his pizza. He chews, swallows, and then says, "What I *am* ready to do is get Brandi out of my head. For good. Any advice on how to do that?"

Augie taps his mini Bible again. "James 5:16 tells us, 'Confess your sins to one another and pray for one another, that you may be healed.' The way I see it, you can either let anger and resentment build up inside you, Mark, or reach out to Brandi with repentance, humility, and love."

Mark makes a face. "I've tried reaching out to her, like, a million times. She doesn't want anything to do with me!"

Augie shrugs. "Have you tried reaching out to apologize?"

CHAPTER 16

BRANDI McCLAIN STILL CAN'T BELIEVE she's going through with this.

Her mother, her stepfather, her friends—they all said she was crazy. And maybe, on some level, she is.

But tonight, standing on her parents' front steps as Mark Rogowski pulls his car into the driveway, Brandi waves, walks over, and gets in the passenger seat.

Just a few days ago, something like this would have been unimaginable to her. But that was before she received Mark's long, thoughtful, handwritten letter.

At first reluctant to open it, Brandi expected it to be a string of threats, insults, and profanities. Instead it was an earnest peace offering and a heartfelt apology. Mark was asking her to look into her heart and forgive him for his many past sins and transgressions. Would she consider sharing one last meal with him, so the two could have a final air-clearing conversation? In exchange, he promised to stop bothering her forever.

After being stalked, harassed, and tormented by Mark for months, Brandi could scarcely believe what she was reading. His words flooded her with relief—and hope.

Maybe Mark really was feeling remorseful. Maybe he really was going to leave her alone, once and for all. Maybe, she thought, just maybe she could finally stop looking over her shoulder everywhere she went, stop tensing up every time the phone rang.

If having one last meal together was what it would take, Brandi decided—after a good deal of reflection—it would be worth it.

"You look really pretty tonight, baby," Mark says.

"Thanks," she answers evenly. To make room for her legs, she pushes aside the red metal Club—the steering wheel–locking anti-theft device—that's resting on the floor mat. "But I'd appreciate it if you didn't call me that."

"Come on, I was just being nice. Relax."

"I'm *very* relaxed, thank you. But I'm not your baby anymore, Mark. Maybe some other women in your life like it when you call them that, but—"

"There *are* no other chicks in my life, Brandi. You know that. I'm saving myself for marriage. If you'd been cool with that, maybe we'd still be together."

Brandi sighs. They haven't even left her driveway yet and already she's starting to have second thoughts.

"Fine. Whatever. Can we just go to the restaurant?"

But the car doesn't budge.

"First, let's talk about *your* sex life for a second."

"*Excuse* me?"

"I haven't seen you with that meathead surfer bro in a while. Are you two still screwing around, or have you already tossed him aside and moved on to the next guy?"

Brandi scowls, shocked and insulted. Her rebound

relationship has indeed been cooling off, but she snarls at Mark, "That is none of your goddamn business."

"Language!" Mark fires back. "Don't ever take the Lord's name in vain like that. Show some respect."

Brandi throws up her hands. "Are you kidding me right now? You're seriously gonna lecture me on Christian values and respect after calling me a slut?"

"I didn't call you—"

"I thought you wanted to apologize. To ask for my forgiveness. To move on."

"I'm trying to, Brandi! But the idea of you being with another guy—"

"*Tough,* Mark. Deal with it. Your jealousy is not my problem. Maybe this was a bad idea." Brandi folds her arms.

"No, no, you're right," Mark says, nodding and calming down. "I'm sorry. For everything. Can we still have one nice last dinner together? Please?"

Ignoring the little voice in her head screaming at her not to go, Brandi agrees.

A few minutes later, she and Mark head out past the guardhouse and turn onto the main road that slices through the foothills around Canyon Lake. As they drive, Brandi can't help but ask, "How'd you do it, by the way? Get past security. I'm curious."

"Uh, it was easy. I told the guy I was here to pick you up. He called your—"

"Not tonight," Brandi interrupts. "The time you snuck into my bedroom and smashed that picture of us and took back all the clothes and jewelry and the Benz you gave me."

Mark is silent for a moment. Then he says, "I don't know what you're talking about. Somebody broke into your folks' place and stole your car? When?"

Now Brandi is quiet, too. How can she possibly respond to what feels to her like such a brazen lie?

She finally settles on "Mark, you're a real asshole. You can hide behind your new religion and your new friends all you want, but at the end of the day—"

Suddenly, Mark slams on the brakes and makes a sharp, squealing left turn onto a dirt road that's nearly hidden behind a giant tree.

"Whoa, what the hell?!" Brandi exclaims. "What are you doing?"

Mark doesn't answer. He keeps his eyes glued to the dark, bumpy, curvy road ahead. The car starts to pick up speed.

So does Brandi's pulse.

"Mark, slow down! Where are you going? If you think this is a shortcut out of the canyon or something, trust me, it's—"

Mark brakes hard again. The car comes to a rough, skidding stop in the middle of this dark, quiet road surrounded by dense trees.

Mark turns to Brandi, his face contorted with rage. In a deep, frightening voice, he screams at her, "You know what I should do?! I should take you out to the desert right now! I should beat the shit out of you and leave you there! And I would get away with it, because everybody would know you deserved it!"

Brandi sits frozen in the passenger seat.

Stunned by what Mark is saying.

Paralyzed by fear.

"Mark…please…"

"Please *what*?! What do you have to say for yourself?!"

Brandi's whole body starts to tremble. Her eyes well up with tears.

"Please…don't hurt me…"

Mark balls up his fists and leans in close. Brandi can smell his sour breath.

"Is that the best you've got?!"

"I'm begging you, Mark...please...My mother knows where I am! If I...If I don't come home tonight..."

Brandi trails off, too upset to finish the sentence.

At last Mark leans back in his seat. He rubs his face with his hands. He mumbles something under his breath that sounds to Brandi like some kind of prayer.

Then he slowly turns the car around and drives her back to her house.

CHAPTER 17

OKAY, WE'RE DOING IT TODAY."

Those are the first and only words Augie Constantino hears Mark Rogowski say on the phone to him one chilly morning.

But he understands exactly what they mean. Within minutes, he hops onto his skateboard and heads over to Mark's condo.

Mark greets him at the door wearing ripped jeans and a black hoodie that reads I SKATE YESTERDAY AND TODAY AND FOREVER, a play on a verse from the Old Testament.

"Hey, dude, thanks for coming over so fast," Mark says.

"What did I tell you? The moment you were ready, I'd be here to help."

Augie follows his friend inside. In the middle of the living room are two flat, unassembled cardboard boxes; they're surrounded by a sea of old magazines and VHS tapes—all with beautiful, buxom women on the covers in various stages of undress.

"Wow. Quite a collection. Is this everything?" Augie asks.

"Almost. Got a little bit more in the bedroom. I figured I could finish going through them while you made the boxes and started packing them up?"

Augie says he'd be happy to, "but first, let's read a bit of scripture together, shall we? I found a passage that reminds me why what we're doing is so important."

With a shrug, Mark agrees. The two sit on the sofa.

Augie opens his pocket Bible, clears this throat, and reads aloud: "Matthew 5:27. 'You have heard it said, "You shall not commit adultery." But I say to you, everyone who looks at a woman with lustful intent has already committed adultery with her in his heart. If your right eye causes you to sin, tear it out and throw it away. For it is better that you lose one of your members than that your whole body be thrown into hell.'"

After Augie finishes the reading—which, strangely, seems to make Mark a little uncomfortable—Mark disappears up the stairs and into his bedroom.

Augie uses a roll of clear packing tape to construct the pair of boxes. Then he starts loading them up with Mark's videos and magazines as fast as he can, like a train engineer shoveling coal into a fiery engine.

Hoping to avoid triggering any "lustful intent" himself, Augie does his best not to read or even look at any of the titles or photographs. At least not too closely.

But despite his efforts, a few covers do catch Augie's attention.

And they give him serious pause.

Paying more attention now, he notices images of naked women locked in cages.

Women shackled to dungeon walls.

Women stretched out, spread-eagle, across medieval torture devices.

Women being held at knifepoint by unseen assailants, looking terrified.

Even women flung across beds and splayed on the ground, their eyes vacant, their bodies splattered with blood, "playing dead" with extraordinary realism.

Augie gasps in shock and hurls the stack he's holding to the floor.

He shuts his eyes and mutters, "Dear Lord in heaven, give me strength..."

Augie is hardly a stranger to pornography. He's looked at more issues of *Playboy* and *Penthouse* than he can remember. He's watched plenty of skin flicks, too.

But Mark's stash?

Augie has never seen anything so dark or twisted in his life.

And he finds it deeply, spiritually disturbing.

"Okay, this is the last of 'em!" Mark announces happily as he reenters the living room. He dumps the armful of smut that he's holding into one of the boxes and then finishes gathering up the rest of his collection strewn around the carpet.

Meanwhile, Augie stands there staring at Mark. Speechless. Uneasy.

"Whatcha lookin' at?" Mark asks with a smirk. "See something you like?"

"Not funny," Augie replies. "Just hurry up and let's get rid of this stuff, okay?"

When both boxes have been filled to the brim, Augie and Mark each lift one and carry them outside. Mark suggests simply leaving them at the curb to be picked up with the trash the following week. But Augie says that's not good enough. He gets Mark to drive to a large dumpster he noticed on his way over; it's outside a residential construction site a few blocks away. They open the lid and drop the boxes inside. They land with a heavy thud.

"Free at last!" Mark exclaims, dusting off his hands. "Thanks again for your help, dude. Hey, want to go grab some breakfast and do some witnessing? I saw a bunch of skaters hanging around a 7-Eleven not far from here the other day. Maybe we mix it up this time, skip the beaches and try there?"

Normally Augie would jump at the idea. But today he politely declines.

After the stream of troubling images he's just seen, all he wants to do is go home, hug his wife, and pray.

Early March, 1991

MARK ROLLS OVER WITH A GRUNT. He kicks at his covers. He pounds his pillow.

Glancing at the digital clock radio next to his bed, he sees that it's almost three o'clock in the morning. He's been tossing and turning for hours, unable to fall asleep.

It started about six weeks ago, and it's been happening almost every night.

Mark feels as though his mind is on fire. He can't stop thinking about the state of his life. About how much living he's done in his twenty-four years. About how much everything has changed, and how quickly. How much he's gained by dedicating himself to Jesus, but how much he's had to suffer and lose along the way. His career. His fame. His fortune. His friends.

And of course his girlfriend.

Even all these months after their breakup, picturing Brandi McClain still fills Mark with a deep, indescribable longing.

And imagining her sleeping with other men triggers a vast, simmering rage.

Just because Mark asked Brandi for forgiveness doesn't mean that he's forgiven *her*. Not by a mile. He's still incensed when he thinks back to how closed-minded she was about his religious rebirth, especially after all they'd been through. How she refused to convert, or even entertain the idea of going to church or staying celibate. How one single, brief, minor physical scuffle one evening was all it took for her to dump him and move out.

And then—within days, practically—she had completely moved on!

To Mark, Brandi hopping into another man's bed so soon after leaving his was the most painful part of all. *She probably did it just to spite me!* he thinks. *And who knows how many other guys she's been with since?*

Mark slams his fists against his mattress. He wants Brandi back, desperately. But he knows he can't have her. Not now. Not ever.

Still, how could that bitch be so cruel?!

That's it. Mark can't take it anymore.

He bolts up in bed and shoots to his feet, knowing exactly what he needs to do.

After pacing his bedroom for a good fifteen minutes, amping himself up, he puts on some clothes, slips out of his condo, and gets in his car.

The drive from Carlsbad to Canyon Lake would normally take around ninety minutes. But in the middle of the night, zooming along the eerily empty freeways, Mark is able to get there in under an hour. As he pulls up to the guardhouse at the entrance to Brandi's mother and stepfather's gated community, a portly security guard appears at the window.

"Can I help you, son?"

"Yeah. My name's Mark Anthony. My friend Brandi McClain lives here. She's got a really early flight out of Lindbergh this morning. She asked me to give her a ride?"

The guard squints at Mark and then flips through pages on a clipboard.

"Last name was 'Anthony,' you said? I don't see you on the guest list."

"Seriously? Come on. I've been here a million times. You can check the log."

The guard frowns. Not buying Mark's bluff. He picks up a phone.

"Just one second. Let me give the McClains a quick call—"

"*Dude*. Do you really want to wake the whole house up at four fifteen in the morning? Look, her flight is in, like, two hours. If she misses it, she's gonna kill *both* of us. Just let me through, okay? Brandi's waiting for me. I'll be in and out in ten minutes, tops."

The security guard hesitates. Then he hangs up the phone. A few seconds later, the metal gate lifts and Mark cruises on through.

Mark soon pulls up, slowly, quietly, in front of Brandi's house. The last time he was here—to pick her up for their aborted dinner date a few weeks ago—she was waiting for him out on the steps. Now she's probably in her bedroom, fast asleep.

And she has no idea he's coming for her.

Mark gets out and approaches the side of the house.

Gazing up at her window now, he visualizes Brandi lying in her bed. Curled up beneath her comforter. Naked, of course. So peaceful. So vulnerable.

Mark shuts his eyes and imagines creeping up next to her.

Reaching out his hands.

Wrapping them around her neck.

Mark savors the twisted fantasy of Brandi choking,

writhing, and gagging as he squeezes, harder and harder. He pictures himself wringing the last drops of life from his bitch of an ex-girlfriend. When it's all over, Mark finally feels a sense of calm. Peace. Freedom.

Mark opens his eyes, *resolving to do it now for real.*

But when he tries to take a step toward the house, his feet won't budge.

It's as if some kind of strong yet invisible spiritual force is stopping him.

Mark tries again. He wills his body to move. To obey his command.

But he remains motionless.

All at once, Mark is overcome by a profound sense of guilt and shame. Tears spring from his eyes. He shuts them again—and this time says a silent prayer, thanking God for holding him back from committing such a horrible, unforgivable act.

Almost miraculously, Mark regains control of his muscles.

He spins on a dime, gets back into his car, and speeds away into the night.

March 20, 1991

TWENTY-ONE-YEAR-OLD Jessica Bergsten hangs her last dress in the closet and zips shut her now-empty suitcase. She can't wait to unpack the rest of her clothes and belongings, but they'll have to stay in boxes and other suitcases until she has a chance to buy furniture.

Looking around the small, sunny apartment she's just moved into, Jessica tries to envision how she's going to decorate—which quickly turns into fantasizing about the exciting new life that lies ahead.

After contemplating the decision for what felt like forever, she's finally made the leap from Arizona to Southern California!

Jessica knows she has so much to do. Jobs to apply for, modeling agents to submit to, new friends to make. But then something dawns on her. She might be able to jump-start all of that with a single phone call.

After rummaging through some cardboard boxes, she digs out her leather-bound address book and makes a call.

On the fifth ring, a man groggily picks up. "Hello?"

"Hi, is this, um...Gator Rogowski?"

"I haven't gone by either of those names in a long time. Who's asking?"

"Oh. It's Jessica. Jessica Bergsten. I'm not sure if you remember me. I'm a good friend of Brandi McClain's. We met at a skate party in Phoenix, like, four years ago?"

After a solid six-second pause, Mark Rogowski exclaims, "Jess! Yeah, of course I remember you. Brandi used to talk about you all the time. How's it going?"

"Really great, Mark, thanks! So, the reason I'm calling is...I know this is a little out of the blue...but I actually just moved to San Diego! I don't really know anybody here, though—besides Brandi, of course. But we haven't talked in, like, forever. I don't even have her number anymore."

"Yeah. Me neither."

"Anyway...I know it's been a while, but I was hoping maybe you and I could grab a bite or something? I'm sure you're super busy, but maybe you could show me around the city, point out some fun places to hang out and party? You always seemed to know all the coolest underground spots."

There's another pause on the line. An even longer one this time.

Then Mark replies, "I'd love to."

Jessica thrusts the cordless phone she's holding into the air and does a short victory dance. After moving to town less than a week ago, she's already hanging out with one of the raddest San Diegans she's ever met!

Mark says he happens to be free that afternoon and suggests they grab lunch. He even offers to pick Jessica up from her new place in Pacific Beach. Jessica says she couldn't be more excited—or grateful.

She's just about finished getting ready—brushing

her shoulder-length blond hair, applying mascara to highlight her bright blue eyes—when she hears the friendly toot of a car horn outside.

Mark, who's even more handsome now than Jessica remembers, drives them about ten minutes to a cozy Italian bistro along the waterfront in La Jolla. Snagging a parking spot right out front, Mark carefully locks his steering wheel with the Club and then insists on walking around to the passenger side and opening Jessica's door for her. She giggles, enjoying the gentlemanly act.

Over eggplant Parmesan and caprese salad, the two near strangers catch up. By the meal's end, they've practically become old pals. Their conversation flows as easily as the bottle of wine they share.

Jessica is dazzled by Mark's tales of his former pro-skater glory. She's saddened that he and Brandi have broken up and lost touch, but deeply moved by his story of finding religion after his accident in Germany. Her past few years in Arizona, Jessica tells him, haven't been nearly as eventful. She's mostly spent them working a string of part-time jobs and partying. That's a big reason she decided to move to San Diego in the first place: to break out of her routine; to jump-start a new life; and to pursue her dream of modeling, as Brandi did.

"Well, if she can do it, you can, too!" Mark says. "You look just like her. Always have."

Their lunch stretches on for almost two hours, but their day together is just getting started. Mark drives Jessica all over the city, showing her his favorite beaches, bars, parks, hangouts, and of course Calvary Chapel, his beloved church.

At around dusk, Mark invites Jessica to come over and hang at his Carlsbad condo. She's having such a good time with this attractive, charming guy, she couldn't possibly say no.

They stop to rent some movies and buy a few bottles of wine. Back at his place, Mark pops a cork and then pops in a film. Jessica sits next to him on the sofa—and by the movie's end, she has snuggled up close.

"This has been such a fun day, Mark," Jessica says, yawning and reaching for her purse. "It's getting late...but I really hope we can do it again sometime."

"Me, too, Jess. Me, too."

"Do you think you could give me a ride home?"

For a moment, Mark doesn't answer. He simply stares at Jessica, his expression cloudy and intense. Then, just as suddenly, he brightens.

"Sure. Happy to. But, shit, you know what?" Mark pats the pockets of his jeans. "I think I left my wallet in the car, with my license in it. Why don't you gather up your stuff, and I'll go check and be right back?"

Jessica does so as Mark exits his condo. A few minutes later, she's wandered over to the mantel in his living room to examine some old framed photographs.

"This picture of you skydiving is so awesome, Mark!" she calls to him when she hears the front door open. "I've always wanted to try, but I'm way too—"

Jessica turns to see Mark striding ominously toward her.

He's holding the Club, its red steel glinting under the room's light.

"Mark...?! What are you—oh, my God, no!"

Mark raises the Club and swings with all his might. He makes contact with the back of Jessica's skull. Mark swings again. Then a third time.

Jessica crumples to the living room floor.

CHAPTER 20

MARK TOSSES THE CLUB aside and glares down at Jessica's body, curled up on the floor in a limp, twisted heap.

A stream of blood is flowing from the massive gash on the back of her head, already seeping into the beige living room carpet.

Mark stands there, breathing heavily, his heart rate at a gallop.

Slowly he begins to process the sheer horror of what he's just done—and why.

He can't quite explain it, but it was as if something just came over him. Some kind of force. Blindingly vengeful. Ineffably evil.

Looking at Jessica just a few minutes ago, he felt completely overwhelmed by it.

And in that moment, Mark saw a brief but vivid flash of Brandi.

Not surprisingly, since the two women resemble each other in so many ways. Both are tall and thin. Both are blond and beautiful.

And both, Mark thinks, are sneakily seductive. Sinful. Wicked. Sacrilegious.

Jessica...Brandi...Jessica...Brandi... In Mark's twisted mind, in that split second, the two women became one and the same.

All his pent-up jealousy, rage, and pain exploded.

"Look what you made me do!" Mark roars at Jessica's crumpled body. "Both of you!" Thanks to his stupid ex, this poor other girl, a person he barely knows, is...

Wait. Is she moving?

Incredibly, Jessica appears to still be—just barely—alive.

Mark watches as she wheezes and whimpers, twitches and squirms.

As she does, his eyes wander slowly up and down the aspiring model's slender, enticing body.

Another powerful force begins to stir inside him.

In a second fit of fury, Mark bends down, scoops Jessica into his arms—and then hauls her across the living room, up the stairs, and into his bedroom.

He flings her unconscious body onto his bed and then rummages around a box in the back of his closet until he finds what he's looking for.

A pair of metal handcuffs and a set of leather shackles.

Mark stretches out Jessica's limbs and binds them to the bedposts.

Then he cuts off all her clothes with a pair of scissors.

Mark rapes Jessica—over and over, again and again. Over the next several hours, he commits every sex act he can imagine upon her defenseless body. Sometimes he pictures images from his deviant porn collection. Sometimes he thinks it's Brandi he's punishing. Other times, his mind hazy and warped, Mark barely thinks about anything at all.

For most of the horrific ordeal, Jessica is passed out, or semiconscious.

And then she starts to wake up.

Despite the unimaginable agony she must be in, Jessica begs Mark to stop. She implores him to uncuff her, to let her go. Please. *Please*.

But Mark doesn't *want* to let her go. In fact, Jessica's cries only make him angrier. More driven. More sadistic in his desire to take out his violent revenge on this innocent stand-in.

Soon Jessica's pleas turn to screams—desperate and primal.

Mark tries to muffle her mouth with one hand, but it's no use. She continues crying out for help at the top of her lungs.

He checks the digital clock radio by his bed. He's been raping Jessica for nearly three full hours. It's now the middle of the night—and if she doesn't shut up soon, Mark is afraid the neighbors will call the cops.

Mark gets up from his bed, returns to his closet, and grabs an oversize surfboard bag.

He unlocks Jessica's handcuffs and shackles, but before she can escape, he shoves her nude body off the bed and into the bag.

Panicking, Jessica yells louder than ever, using every last drop of her strength to try fighting Mark off—thrashing, kicking, clawing.

But it's no use.

Straddling his terrified victim, Mark places one hand over her mouth and another around her throat. He squeezes both tightly. Gradually, Jessica stops resisting.

As her last gasp escapes, Mark removes his hands and stares down at her bloody, battered body.

This time, he's certain of it.

Jessica Bergsten is dead.

He's killed her, just as he fantasized about murdering Brandi.

Mark zips up the surfboard bag, gets dressed, and hauls Jessica's body downstairs. He has to get rid of all the evidence. Fast. Making sure the coast is clear, he exits his condo and stuffs the bag and the other evidence into his car trunk.

Mark doesn't have a plan at this point—except to drive as fast and as far away from here as he can, in search of the perfect dumping ground.

He spends the next two hours in a feverish haze, cruising on mental autopilot along a series of freeways. He heads south and then east, away from the sprawl of San Diego and toward the vast, craggy, punishing U.S.-Mexico borderlands.

There's no particular reason Mark pulls off the sleepy two-lane desert highway when he does. He doesn't know this patch of dirt better than any other for hundreds of miles in either direction. But he does know that dawn will be breaking soon. *Better to bury the body here,* he thinks, *under cover of darkness, than go further out in daylight.*

Mark parks, lifts the bag out of his trunk, and drags Jessica's body along the rocky sand. Just before reaching a small ravine off a dry riverbed, he uses his bare hands to scoop out a shallow grave.

Then he unzips the surfboard bag and dumps Jessica's naked corpse into the grave.

Back on the freeway now, speeding home, Mark tosses blood-splattered evidence—his clothes, the surfboard bag, and his Club—out the window at separate, random intervals.

But what to do about his blood-soaked apartment?

With the sun already peeking over the horizon,

Mark passes a twenty-four-hour grocery store and gets an idea.

He pulls over and pops inside to rent a carpet steamer.

Back at his condo, Mark immediately gets to work. After a few hours of fastidious, frantic scrubbing, wiping, scouring, and bleaching, every inch of his place is spotless.

Exhausted, drained, and shell-shocked, Mark collapses onto his couch.

Shutting his eyes, he starts to pray, the weight of what he's done only now slowly sinking in.

In a matter of hours, Mark has gone from a follower of Christ to a killer of women.

CHAPTER 21

Early April, 1991

STEPPING OFF THE PLANE at Lindbergh Field, Stephen Bergsten is hit with a crushing feeling of both urgency and dread.

It's been less than a month since his daughter Jessica moved to San Diego—and over two weeks since anyone has seen or heard from her.

As he beelines to the kiosk to pick up his rental car, Stephen thinks back to late March, when Jessica first failed to return their calls. At first he wasn't overly concerned, recalling how when he was Jessica's age, chatting on the phone with his stuffy old parents wasn't on his priority list, either, and certainly wouldn't have been if he was also in the middle of moving to a new city, starting a new life. But the Bergstens quickly became alarmed enough about being unable to track Jessica down that on March 29, 1991, they filed a missing person report with the San Diego County Sheriff's Department.

Although Stephen would follow up with the California authorities constantly, sometimes multiple times a day, he was also dealing with other problems in

Arizona. A powerful Tucson attorney, he recently learned that one of his biggest clients is facing a major investigation by an Arizona criminal drug task force, and rumors have been swirling that Stephen himself would be under federal investigation for money laundering. It's all a bunch of baloney, but it's been weighing on his mind.

Frustrated because, time after time, the San Diego County Sheriff's Department has told him that they still have zero leads in the case, Stephen decided to fly to California to look for Jessica himself.

Despite being a lawyer, not a private investigator, Stephen knows the importance of gathering solid evidence. So his first stop is Jessica's new apartment. After convincing the landlord to let him in, he gets a little choked up seeing how spare and empty the place still is. A couple of suitcases. Some cardboard boxes. Hardly any furniture. His daughter's new life here has barely begun.

Walking into the kitchen, Stephen notices that one of the only items Jessica seems to have unpacked is her leather-bound address book. It's sitting on the ground by the phone, open to the *G* section. Stephen skims the page. There's only one entry that isn't for a friend or acquaintance in Arizona. Written in Jessica's swooping cursive scrawl is the name Gator, followed by a San Diego address and phone number.

"Sorry, Mr. B., I don't know where she is."

Stephen stands at the front door of a Carlsbad apartment, where a lanky, bedraggled skater punk wearing a crucifix around his neck tells him that no, he hasn't seen Jessica recently.

"But you said you saw her a few weeks ago?" Stephen asks, guardedly hopeful.

"Yeah. She called me. Said she'd just moved here and didn't know anyone. We grabbed some lunch, then we said good-bye. That was it."

"And when was this exactly?"

"Like I told you. A couple weeks ago."

"*When?!* I need to know precisely—it's important! There's a chance you might be the last person who saw my daughter alive. So think, damn it!"

"Whoa—relax, dude! That's the best I got. And a 'Thank you' might be nice."

Stephen stews. He digs his nails into his fists to keep himself from punching this snarky son of a bitch in the face. He came all the way over here hoping for some concrete information about his daughter. Instead all he's gotten is attitude.

"I'm trying to find my little girl," he hisses, stepping in close to the young man. "And you want me to *thank* you? For wasting my time?!"

"Forget it, Pops," says the skater punk with a dismissive flick of his wrist. Before slamming the door in Stephen's face, he adds, "Have a blessed day."

Stephen gulps down his fury and gets back in his rental car. He heads to his next destination: a printshop downtown.

He called ahead and made an appointment with a designer, who is now helping him create a simple black-and-white flyer with Jessica's photo, along with her birthday, height, weight, and hair and eye color.

Stephen dabs his eyes as he hands over the recent picture he and his wife picked out. In it, Jessica is standing alone in their kitchen. Her head is tilted slightly upward, her long blond locks cascading over her left shoulder. A carefree smile beams across her angelic face.

Once he's been handed a stack of a few thousand flyers, Stephen gets back in his rental car. He plans to spend the next few days crisscrossing San Diego, sticking them to every telephone pole, in every store window, and under every set of windshield wipers in the city.

But first he leans forward, rests his head against the steering wheel, and weeps.

Desperately hoping his little girl is still alive.

Terrified he may be too late.

CHAPTER 22

April 10, 1991

AT THIS HOUR, RALPH SMITH, a coroner investigator with the Imperial County Sheriff's Office, would normally be heading home to have dinner with his wife and children. But today he knows he'll be lucky if he makes it home before breakfast.

It's going to be a very long night.

Driving west along Interstate 8, Smith takes in the final few moments of the stunning sunset, the sky a vibrant fuchsia and tangerine. Twenty minutes later, turning off the highway and onto a long, dusty dirt road, he sees red and blue: the flashing emergency lights of a fire truck, an ambulance, and five police cars parked up ahead.

Smith pulls his white coroner's van to a stop nearby. He shows his credentials to a middle-aged sheriff's deputy, who leads him on foot even deeper into the desert flats.

"A father and son found the remains a couple hours ago," says the deputy.

"What were they doing all the way out here?"

"Rented some ATVs. Family vacation. They sped back into town and called it in."

"That's too bad. Nothing ruins a holiday like finding a dead body."

"Body?" the deputy says grimly. "Not exactly."

The two soon reach a group of other uniformed deputies and plainclothes detectives, all clustered near a small ravine. Portable floodlights have been set up to illuminate this otherwise pitch-black patch of desert.

After covering his brown leather loafers with blue protective booties and slipping on white latex gloves, Smith ducks under a strip of yellow police tape and begins to survey the scene.

A human skeleton is lying supine in the sand.

Its extremities are outstretched. Its marble-white skull is tilted slightly to the left. Its jaw is dangling open.

Smith shuts his eyes for just a few seconds—his private way of paying the dead the briefest moment of respect—and sets to work.

Drawing on his years of education and experience, he pads slowly around the remains, taking in all angles, crouching from time to time to inspect them more closely.

The first thing Smith notices is that the bones are remarkably intact. That's not surprising given the area's hot, dry climate, but it's still a rare sight to see.

The next thing Smith observes is that the remains are female, his trained forensic eye quickly homing in on the more rounded mandible, the narrower shoulder girdle, the shorter rib cage, and the wider pelvic opening.

"Any idea how he went?" asks the deputy, watching Smith from a few feet away.

"She," Smith corrects him. "And no. Won't know for sure until the autopsy, but I don't see any obvious signs of foul play. No gunshot wound. No broken bones."

"You're saying she died of natural causes? Come on."

"At this point? It's too early to say much of *anything*."

But he can make a couple of educated deductions. Based on the state of the sutures in the woman's skull—the jagged lines where bone plates grow more tightly fused as a person ages—Smith presumes that the woman was between eighteen and twenty-five years old when she died. And if he had to guess without measuring, he'd say she probably stood between five seven and five nine.

"How long do you think she's been out here?" asks the deputy.

"Weeks at least. Maybe months. Hard to know for certain."

The deputy frowns, frustrated. "So who is she? Will we ever find out?"

Smith is about to answer—to say that, though far from guaranteed, sometimes IDs can be made using dental records—when he stops, leans in closer to the remains, and lifts an eyebrow.

To his surprise, he now sees that the woman's feet, one calf, and both hands appear to be partially preserved. There may even be enough mummified skin remaining that Smith can manage to lift some usable fingerprints back at his lab.

"We don't know who she is *yet,*" Smith answers the deputy. "But I have a feeling we will soon."

His initial inspection complete, Smith stands and marches back to his van. He's got photos to take, paperwork to fill out, calls to make. He's looking at at least a few more hours of work here on scene, and still more once the body is transported to the morgue. No way he's going to get to see his kids tonight before they go to sleep.

But they may just catch a glimpse of *him*.

As he nears his vehicle, Smith spots a second van farther down the road: a news van from a local San Diego affiliate. A cameraman and female reporter are already filming and speaking with a senior deputy.

Clearly word of the skeleton's discovery has already started to spread. And if Smith's years of working as a coroner have taught him anything, finding decomposed remains—especially those belonging to a young woman—is always a very big story.

CHAPTER 23

Early May, 1991

HEY, DO YOU GUYS HAVE A few minutes to hear about the Lord?"

Standing outside a 7-Eleven in Carlsbad, Augie Constantino is trying to talk to a mixed-gender group of teenagers exiting the store.

"Get lost," one of them says.

"I *used* to be lost. But then I found my way. Through God." Augie holds out a business card. "Here. If any of you ever need someone to talk to, I run a youth crisis hotline out of the basement of my church."

"Bro, the only crisis I see is your haircut!"

The teens snicker and move on. Augie sighs, disappointed but undeterred—especially when he spots Mark Rogowski riding toward him on his skateboard.

"You're late, man!" Augie yells to him, jokingly.

"I thought our souls were eternal. What's the rush?"

The two friends laugh, hug, and set about witnessing together, here at one of their new favorite spots.

About an hour later, a sun-kissed brunette who looks to be in her early twenties exits the convenience store carrying a bright red slushy and a salted soft pretzel.

She's wearing a tank top and a tiny miniskirt—or a "towel," as Augie likes to call such scandalously skimpy articles of clothing.

Both Augie and Mark notice the young woman right away. Mark puts on a charming smile and starts to approach. But Augie holds out his hand: *I got this one*.

"Excuse me, miss?" Augie politely calls to her. "Why don't you go put some more clothes on, and when you come back, I'd like to talk to you about Christ."

The young woman recoils. "What did you just say to me?"

Augie backpedals. "I...I'm sorry. I didn't mean to insult you. But you're wearing a provocative outfit, and we live in an evil world. I'm worried about you—that's all."

"Yeah, well, don't be. I'm just fine. I don't need Jesus in my life. I don't have a thing to worry about."

Augie points to the phone booth in front of the 7-Eleven. Its outside is plastered with papers, ads, and flyers, all fluttering in the ocean breeze.

"Oh, really?" he asks. "What about *that* girl?"

One of the posters, tattered and faded from days in the sun, says MISSING PERSON. Beneath the text is a picture of a pretty young blonde, smiling big, and beneath that, a phone number and address to contact for any information.

"That girl," Augie continues, "probably thought she had nothing to worry about, either." Earnest and ardent, his voice begins to rise. "But where is she now? She could have gotten involved in drugs! Pornography! Maybe she's dead!"

The miniskirt girl waves Augie away like a gnat. "Maybe you should mind your own business, you creep," she says, and then gets into a nearby car and drives off.

Augie sighs deeply and shakes his head. "When did having some modesty become such a terrible thing? And how about showing a little compassion for a missing girl in need—a girl in *trouble*?"

Augie turns back to Mark, expecting agreement.

Instead he sees his friend staring vacantly at the missing person poster.

"You okay there, buddy?" Augie asks.

"Huh? Yeah, I'm fine," Mark says after a few seconds. "Completely fine."

Augie isn't convinced but doesn't push it. Instead he walks over to the phone booth, looks more closely at the flyer, and then starts to carefully take it down.

"Hey—stop. What are you doing?" Mark asks, a hint of distress in his voice.

"I want to remember to pray for her later," Augie replies. "Her name is Jessica. And wherever she may be, she could use some extra love and grace."

Augie gently folds the sheet into quarters and places it between two pages of his red-leather Bible.

Mark watches with what appears to be growing discomfort and then drops his skateboard. "Screw this," he scoffs. "I'm going home."

Augie is very much taken aback by his friend's unexpected reaction, and can only watch in confusion as Mark keeps skating away.

CHAPTER 24

Later that week

'WHEN JUDAS, WHO HAD BETRAYED him, saw that Jesus was condemned, he was seized with remorse and returned the thirty pieces of silver to the chief priests and the elders.'"

Augie looks at the intimate group of Calvary Chapel worshippers seated around his living room this afternoon. All, including him, are holding a Bible.

"Who'd like to continue?" he asks. "Mark?"

Mark clears his throat and reads aloud: "'"I have sinned," he said, "for I have"'"—he shifts in his seat—"'"for I have betrayed innocent blood." "What is that to us?" they replied. "That's your responsibility." So Judas threw the money into the temple and left. Then he went away...and hanged himself.'"

Augie nods a thanks to Mark and closes his Bible. Then he asks the room, "Now why do you think Judas reacted the way he did when he learned Jesus would be crucified, and how can this story help us live our own lives?"

For the next thirty minutes, the group engages in a thoughtful conversation about this controversial biblical figure. They discuss the meaning of Judas's betrayal. His possible possession by the devil. And ultimately, his suicide.

At one point, Augie refers to Judas as "the great pretender," because while the apostle might have claimed to be a follower of Jesus, clearly that was a big, fat lie.

"Personally, I think it's completely normal to have spiritual doubts," Augie says, "to question the teachings of scripture. But to betray Christ on such a deep level? That's a step too far. And look what happened to Judas. I think someone upstairs agreed."

The Bible study group ends, but as everyone files out, Augie pulls Mark aside.

"You doing okay, brother?" he asks warmly. "You're usually such an active participant in our group. You seemed pretty quiet tonight. Something on your mind?"

Mark stammers a bit and then says, "Sorry. Nah, I'm all good. Just tired, I guess."

Augie looks closely at his friend, trying to get a read on him. He can tell that something's been troubling Mark. But he can't figure out what.

"Would you like to stay for dinner? We're making spaghetti and meat—"

"Italian? Uh...no...I can't. But thanks, Augie. Maybe another time."

Later that night, at around eleven o'clock, Augie and his wife are getting ready for bed when they hear a thunderous pounding on their front door.

Augie cautiously goes to open the door. To his shock, standing there is Mark, looking like an absolute mess. His hair is disheveled. His face is puffy and red. His cheeks are streaked with tears. And his breath reeks of alcohol.

"Mark?! What happened?"

"Hey, dude," Mark says with a sniffle. Looking both dazed and jumpy, disoriented and on edge, he wanders inside and sinks down on Augie's couch.

"I'm Judas, Augie!" he wails. "That's what happened. I'm Judas Iscariot!"

Augie hurries over and sits next to Mark. "What do you mean, you're Judas? What are you talking about?"

But Mark doesn't answer. He rests his head in his hands and starts to sob.

"It's all right, Mark. Everything's going to be okay," Augie says, still confused but trying to be reassuring. "Why don't we pray together? Maybe that will make you feel better." Augie takes Mark's hand and says, "Our Father in heaven, hallowed be your name. Your kingdom come, your will be done..."

By the end of the Lord's Prayer, Mark does indeed seem calmer and more grounded. He wipes his nose. He blots his eyes.

And comes clean.

"So...you know that skeleton they found near Ocotillo that was on the news a couple weeks ago? And you know the missing girl on that flyer at 7-Eleven? Well...that was me."

Augie tilts his head. "I don't understand. *What* was you?"

"I'm saying that skeleton belongs to the girl they've been looking for. Jessica Bergsten. And I know that because...I did it. I did it, Augie, okay? I confess! I snapped and I attacked her. I raped her. I murdered her. Then I drove a couple hours and dumped her body in the desert."

Augie is dumbstruck. What Mark is saying is so awful, so outrageous, it can't possibly be true. Can it?

"I betrayed everything and everyone I love!" Mark

moans. "But most of all, I betrayed Christ. Don't you see? I'm a pretender just like Judas—only worse!"

"Oh, Mark!" Augie exclaims, wrapping his friend in a tight embrace. "Christ still loves you. *I* still love you. I'm here for you, now and always. Let's go to the police, tell them what happened—"

"The police? No way. They'll lock me up forever!"

"Mark, you have to turn yourself in. It's the only way. But forever on earth will be over in the blink of an eye. The only judge you need to worry about is God."

Mark slumps back on the couch, soaking in Augie's words. As he does, a faint train whistle echoes nearby: Augie lives just a few blocks from the tracks.

Suddenly, Mark blurts out, "I can't do this!"

He leaps to his feet, turns, and bolts out of Augie's apartment.

This catches Augie completely by surprise. He calls after Mark, but to no avail. So, despite wearing only boxers and a T-shirt and no shoes or socks, Augie shoots to his feet and chases after Mark.

Outside, Augie sees his friend sprinting down the block toward the tracks. The railroad crossing bell is ringing. The lights are flashing. The gate is down.

The train is barreling in their direction.

"Mark! No!"

But Mark doesn't slow. So Augie increases his speed. He's gaining on Mark. He's getting closer. Closer.

Finally, just a few yards before the crossing, Augie pounces on Mark, tackling him to the concrete. Mark flails wildly, trying to free himself, but Augie holds tight.

Once the train passes, Augie releases Mark. Both men are shaken, panting. "What were you thinking?!" Augie cries.

Mark hangs his head in shame. "You're right," he says. "Maybe...maybe I *should* go to the cops."

"Amen!" Augie answers. "The truth, Mark, will always set you free. *Always*."

CHAPTER 25

May 7, 1991

EVERY COP HAS A STRESS RELIEVER of one kind or another. It's practically a job requirement. Some drink. Some smoke. Some gamble.

Carlsbad police detective Richard Castaneda, a heavyset man with close-cropped black hair and aviator-style eyeglasses, likes to whittle.

He keeps a small pocketknife on him at all times, and the glove box of his unmarked sedan is filled with small wooden carvings in progress. He's found that keeping his hands busy is the perfect way to pass time, especially when he's staking out a suspect or person of interest.

As he's doing right now, parked outside a sports bar near Tamarack Beach.

After weeks of working the Jessica Bergsten case, chasing down possible leads—all of which were dead ends—Castaneda has recently received a promising new tip. A cocktail server noticed one of the flyers Jessica's father wallpapered the city with, and she thinks the victim might have stopped in her bar on the night she went missing.

Castaneda is carefully shaping a wooden hummingbird's wing when he sees a young woman he believes to be the waitress in question approach the bar's entrance. The detective puts away his carving, approaches the possible witness, smooths out his tie, and flashes his badge.

"Excuse me. Are you Wendy? I'm Detective Castaneda. We spoke on the phone."

"Yes. Right. Thanks for meeting me. I really hope I can help."

She can't.

After they chat for a few minutes at a booth inside the bar, it becomes clear to the veteran investigator that the waitress remembers virtually no helpful details at all about her possible interaction with Jessica. Which is completely understandable. The victim was one of a hundred customers Wendy served on an otherwise uneventful Wednesday night almost two months ago.

Castaneda grows even more discouraged when he shows the waitress additional photographs of Jessica, which were provided to the police by the victim's family. He hoped they would jog her memory. Instead they only cause her to doubt her recollection even more. The bar was dark, the waitress explains. Packed with thin blond women, as always. Maybe, she says apologetically, she didn't see Jessica Bergsten after all?

Castaneda gets back into his vehicle, weary and frustrated.

Missing person cases are always challenging—and, sadly, are rarely solved if they stretch on for more than a few days. Castaneda knows, statistically, that at this point Jessica is unlikely to be found alive, if at all. But he's a professional. He isn't giving up, and he never will. For her family's sake, for justice's sake…

His car radio crackles. Castaneda's ears prick up

when he unexpectedly hears his unit number: "One Lincoln seven, ten ninety-five. Code two central. Over."

The dispatcher is informing Castaneda that a subject has been placed into custody, and the detective is ordered to return to headquarters immediately. It's a highly unusual request, and not one Castaneda was expecting. He picks up his radio and responds, "One Lincoln seven, ten four. I'm on my way."

Walking into the station bullpen some fifteen minutes later, Castaneda is intercepted by Detective Don De Tar, who has also been working the Bergsten case.

"So what's the big news, Donny? Did we catch the Zodiac Killer or something?"

De Tar, dry and no-nonsense, steers Castaneda down a hall toward the station's interrogation room.

"Not unless he started murdering folks when he was a baby. We got a twenty-four-year-old white male who walked in the front door about two o'clock. Gave his name as Mark Anthony, but his ID says Rogowski. Apparently, he's some kind of retired pro skateboarder. Showed up with a guy he calls his 'spiritual adviser.'"

"Is that a cute way of saying a lawyer?"

"If it is, the kid needs a better one. He waived his Miranda rights. Said he wanted to talk about Jessica Bergsten. He's claiming he raped and killed her. And those unidentified remains they found in Imperial County last month? He says that's her."

The news literally takes Castaneda's breath away.

Could this really be the break in the case they've been working toward for so long?

Or, with both stories in the news lately, could this guy be just some wacko yanking their chain, a troublemaker hoping for a little free publicity?

"Do you believe him?" Castaneda asks warily. "Or do you think he's full of it?"

He and De Tar arrive at the interrogation room door. "Let's find out."

CHAPTER 26

MARK ROGOWSKI SITS UP straighter when two detectives enter the chilly, austere little room he's been put into. He spoke to one of them earlier; he doesn't recognize the other.

"Mr. Rogowski? I'm Detective Castaneda. You've already met my colleague, Detective De Tar. I'd like to remind you: You still have the right to remain silent. Anything you say to us can and will—"

"I'm done staying quiet, dude," Mark interrupts. "I want to confess."

"All right. Just remember: You can change your mind at any time. You also have the right to have an attorney present. If you can't afford one—"

"Nope. I don't need one. I answer to a higher power. Not an earthly one."

The detectives seem to accept that with a shrug. They take seats at the metal table across from Mark, start rolling a tape recorder, and begin their questioning.

"Why don't you take us through what happened from the beginning?"

And so he does. In eerily calm, detached, painstaking detail, Mark tells the detectives everything.

How Jessica called him one day in March to get lunch and explore the city.

How they went back to his place later to drink wine and watch movies.

How he'd been feeling such jealousy and anger toward his ex-girlfriend, Brandi McClain.

How he'd driven to Brandi's house the previous week with thoughts of killing her.

How Jessica, truly through no fault of her own, became a stand-in for his ex-girlfriend that night, simply because the two women happened to bear a resemblance to each other and have some shared history.

How he lost control, attacked Jessica with the Club, and then shackled and raped her for hours.

How he stuffed her into a surfboard bag and strangled her to keep her quiet.

How he drove for two hours with her body in his trunk, tossing evidence out the window, and then buried her in a shallow grave in a desert ravine in Shell Canyon.

Through all his recounting, Castaneda and De Tar keep relatively straight faces. But this last bit of info Mark shares gets the biggest reaction from them.

"You said…Shell Canyon?" asks De Tar. "Can you be more specific?"

"Yeah. I was going east on Interstate 8. I pulled over, dragged the body south, like, a few hundred yards over the sand. That's when I saw some kinda dried riverbed or something. It looked like a pretty hidden spot, so I buried her next to that."

The two detectives share a look.

"What?" Mark asks. "Did I say something wrong?"

"That's one hell of an understatement," says De Tar under his breath.

Castaneda leans forward. "You did great, Mark. You told us details that were deliberately withheld from the press about where an unidentified body was discovered. You knew things only the real killer could possibly know."

"Now I'm going to go make some calls to our colleagues in Imperial County," De Tar says. "Let them know what's going on."

Castaneda adds, "They'll probably try to confirm whether the Jane Doe they got is Jessica. Then they may have some additional questions for you. Would that be okay with you?"

Mark nods. "I'll do anything I can that's helpful."

Castaneda rises. "In that case, please stand, face the wall, and put your hands behind your back."

Dutifully, Mark obeys.

"Mark Anthony Rogowski, you are under arrest for the rape and murder of Jessica Kay Bergsten."

CHAPTER 27

TURNING ONTO PALM TREE-LINED Garfield Street, a caravan of Carlsbad Police Department vehicles comes to a stop in front of a row of two-story, putty-gray beachside condominiums.

As numerous uniformed officers position their squad cars to block access to the road and other officers begin stringing yellow police tape around the area, Detective Don De Tar leads a team of investigators and crime scene techs onto the property.

"Police department! Search warrant!" he hollers, banging on the front door of Mark Rogowski's condo.

He's well aware that suspect Rogowski is, at present, in custody at a county jail some ten miles away. In theory, the apartment should be empty. But rules are rules, and the department's knock-and-announce policy applies to the execution of virtually all search warrants.

After waiting a few seconds and getting no response, he signals to an officer, who uses a crowbar to wrench open the door.

De Tar and his team stream inside.

Based on the lurid, gory details Rogowski shared during his interrogation about his assault on Jessica Bergsten, his apartment must have looked like a slaughterhouse when it was over.

But today, seven weeks later, the place is spotless. There doesn't seem to be a single shred of evidence anywhere. The carpets, the walls, the furniture—everything looks orderly and pristine.

At least to the naked eye.

De Tar has been in situations like this before. And he has a few tricks up his sleeve to make even the most immaculately bleached crime scene give up its secrets. If Bergsten was beaten and murdered here as Rogowski claims, there will be forensic evidence to prove it.

And damned if De Tar and his team aren't going to find it.

He directs the CSI techs—identifiable by their white full-body jumpsuits and face masks—to spread out and begin their evidentiary collection process.

For the next three hours, they meticulously swab for fluids. Dust for prints. Comb for fibers and hairs.

Once this initial stage has been completed—and proves fruitless—they move on to phase two, which involves some very clever chemistry.

The techs use handheld spray bottles to douse almost every inch of the apartment with diluted luminol. This pale-yellow crystalline substance is known to react with even trace amounts of certain proteins in human blood that are otherwise invisible to the human eye, and which would require professional, heavy-duty, laboratory-grade chemicals to fully wash away.

Once all the surfaces have been evenly wet, the techs draw the blinds, set up a special slow-exposure camera, and shine a high-powered black light.

"Sweet Jesus," De Tar whispers, appalled.

The apartment glows brighter than a planetarium.

The living room carpet, the stairs, the bedroom carpet, and the mattress are all covered with giant fluorescent-blue stains and Jackson Pollock–esque splatters.

When techs later pull up the carpet for a closer look, they see that the victim lost so much blood that it actually soaked through to the padding and wood floors underneath.

There's no other way of describing it.

This is one of the most gruesome crime scenes De Tar has ever seen in his entire career. Even some of the clinical, normally unflappable techs seem unnerved.

De Tar feels an even greater sympathy for Jessica Bergsten than he did before.

And an even stronger desire to see Mark Rogowski pay.

CHAPTER 28

SLIPPING ON AN OLD PAIR of running shoes, Brandi McClain steps out of her house and starts jogging along the hilly private road she still lives on with her mother and stepfather. It's a hot and humid May afternoon. Hardly the perfect running weather. But Brandi is desperate to try anything that might help her clear her head.

She's still bothered by the unexpected phone call she received a few weeks ago from Jessica Bergsten's dad.

Near tears, Mr. Bergsten told Brandi that Jessica had recently moved to San Diego, but had been missing for over a month. He asked if Brandi had any idea where Jessica might be, which Brandi didn't, but she promised to let him know right away if she heard or thought of anything at all that might help the police find her.

The call left Brandi gutted for many reasons. She was horrified to hear that her old friend had disappeared and might be in serious danger, and heartbroken to learn that Jessica had moved to San Diego—largely to follow in her footsteps, it sounded like—yet hadn't reached out.

And she was all the more upset to realize that was probably because of just how far apart the two had drifted over the last few years.

Back in Arizona, Jessica and Brandi were best friends, as close as sisters, with years of shared history. Jessica was there with Brandi on the fateful night she met Mark Rogowski at a skater party in Phoenix, and she was there for her through the turbulent years of the relationship that followed.

But like many friendships, especially long-distance ones, theirs gradually began to fade. It was neither woman's fault; they never had a falling-out. It just happened.

Still, Brandi can't help but feel god-awful about her missing friend.

And in a weird, indescribable way, slightly responsible for it, too.

So while she's not a religious person by any means—as Mark frequently reminded her—Brandi has been praying ardently for Jessica's safe return.

After barely ten minutes of jogging, Brandi stops, turns around, and heads home. Huffing and puffing through the foothills of Canyon Lake hasn't been relaxing at all.

Back in her parents' kitchen, Brandi pours herself a glass of orange juice and wipes her sweaty face with a towel. She's about to hop in the shower when the phone rings.

"Brandi? Hey, girl. It's George."

George is an aspiring young fashion designer Brandi met at a photo shoot about a year ago. The two have since become close. He's normally bubbly and exuberant, but right now he sounds subdued.

"Hi, George. What's up? Is everything all right?"

"I'm so sorry, Brandi. I'm just so sorry. I don't know what to say."

Brandi is silent, confused. Is he talking about Jessica's disappearance? The missing woman has been so much on Brandi's mind, but she hasn't talked to George about her—how would he know that she and Jessica were once such close friends? Brandi asks, "For what? What are you sorry for?"

"Oh, God. Please...no...I'm not the first one to tell you, am I? You don't know?"

Now Brandi's concern is growing. "Know what?"

George lets out a long, pained breath. "It's Mark. In today's paper. You didn't see?"

Brandi is alarmed, but whatever news story her friend is talking about, she hasn't seen it yet. "No, George. I didn't. What are you talking about? Just spit it out."

"Apparently, Mark has confessed to...to...murder! The cops say he was with this girl and just went crazy. He knocked her out. He raped her. Then he killed her! She was a model from Arizona, like you. Same age and everything. It's just awful."

Brandi feels her whole body begin to grow cold and weak. As if every drop of blood were slowly draining away.

No way, she thinks. *No! It can't be. Impossible.*

"What...What was the girl's name, George?" she asks, unsteadily.

Brandi hears a rustling on the other end: George fumbling with the newspaper.

"Her name...was Jessica. Jessica Bergsten."

Brandi lets out a long, loud, guttural howl.

She drops the phone—and her glass of orange juice, which shatters.

She leans against the kitchen wall—and slowly slides down until her legs are splayed on the tile.

Brandi hunches over and starts to weep, uncontrollably, as wave after powerful wave of emotion crashes over her.

Shock. Disbelief. Horror. Denial. Outrage. Despair.

If only she had called me! Brandi thinks. *If only we were still friends! I could have told her to stay away from Mark, I could have warned her! He was dangerous! I could have told her to run the other way!*

Brandi cries even harder as a new emotion overcomes her.

Guilt.

"It was supposed to be me!" she howls, tears streaming. "Oh, Jessica! I'm so sorry! It was supposed to be me!"

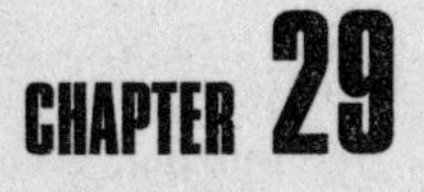

The next day

MARK ROGOWSKI TUGS AT HIS ITCHY, ill-fitting, navy-blue prisoner's jumpsuit. It's a far cry from the stylish duds he's used to wearing. Slouching in the uncomfortable wooden chair, he drums his fingers on the splintery table.

Soon the jail conference-room door opens—and in waddles one of the strangest-looking defense lawyers Mark has ever seen.

Short and rotund, bald on top with a slight mullet, the man appears to be in his thirties. But he's wearing a loud maroon tie and a tan, threadbare, wide-lapeled suit that went out of style during the Nixon administration. He's carrying a bulging briefcase and a black motorcycle helmet emblazoned with the Harley-Davidson logo.

Mark gulps. This is his court-appointed public defender—the only lawyer he was able to get—and the guy doesn't inspire much confidence.

"Mr. Rogowski? I'm John Jimenez," the man barks. "And I'm the only thing standing between you and a needle in your arm. So let's get started."

"Wait—what? Are you serious, dude? Is that really what I'm looking at?!"

"The DA hasn't said yet what sentence they're seeking. And in the end, it's up to the judge to decide—if you're found guilty. But here's the situation."

Jimenez opens his briefcase and starts sifting through files.

"In addition to charging you with kidnapping, rape, use of a deadly weapon, and first-degree murder, the state is trying to add what's called special circumstances. They're saying you killed the victim *during commission* of the rape. Sounds like a minor technicality, right? Wrong. If the judge lets it stand, prosecutors could ask for life without parole…or the death penalty. And they just might get it."

This revelation hits Mark hard.

He's made peace with the fact that he'll likely be facing decades behind bars. Maybe even the rest of his life. But he's okay with that. Part of him even welcomes it. As Augie counseled him, he committed a heinous crime and must atone for his sins. Mark's plan is to serve his time thoughtfully. Spiritually. Studying scripture and witnessing to his fellow inmates.

But execution? That never crossed his mind.

"Okay," Mark says quietly. "I get it. So…what do we do?"

For the next ninety minutes, Jimenez lays out a number of possible defenses.

To begin with, he wants to challenge the validity and admissibility of Mark's confession. Jimenez argues that as Mark's minister, Augie broke his sacred obligation when he drove Mark to the police station and essentially turned him in. Jimenez also says that Augie, by acting as his informal legal adviser, gave Mark misguided advice when he allowed him to speak to the cops without a lawyer present. And the so-called confession, according to Jimenez, is full of leading questions and half-truths. If the judge agrees, the whole thing could be tossed out.

Second, Jimenez wants to cast doubt on the rape itself. Jessica's body is so badly decomposed that he wants to argue there's no way to prove that a forcible sexual assault occurred. With no confession and no physical evidence, the rest of the DA's case could start to look flimsy to a jury, too. At least that's the hope.

Mark listens to his lawyer, resting his chin on tented fingers. He understands the strategy, but he doesn't like it. He doesn't like the idea of going to trial at all—of being judged by twelve flawed mortals like himself.

"What about…some kind of plea deal?" he asks. "Instead of fighting the truth, what if I take responsibility for my actions, and beg for mercy and forgiveness? I believe that's what Christ would want me to do. It's what I believe he'd do himself."

Jimenez leans back and folds his arms.

"I don't think Jesus would ever find himself in the kind of situation you're in, pal. But I hear what you're saying. And you're the defendant. Not me. I can talk to the DA's office about a plea, give it a shot. But no guarantee they'll say yes."

"I understand," Mark says. "I trust you, Mr. Jimenez. But I trust God more."

March 6, 1992

ALL RISE! VISTA SUPERIOR COURT is now in session, the Honorable Thomas J. Whelan presiding."

Mark Rogowski, John Jimenez, and the rest of the courtroom stand at attention as the judge—distinguished and grandfatherly, with neatly styled white hair—enters and takes his seat on the bench.

Judge Whelan flashes a compassionate smile.

But the mood inside his court today couldn't be more tense.

From the lawyers sitting before him, to the Bergsten family in the front row, to the mix of spectators, journalists, and young, rowdy, vibrantly dressed skateboarding fans who have packed the remainder of the gallery, everyone seems on edge.

It doesn't help that Judge Whelan has ordered five additional uniformed bailiffs to stand sentry around the room, on high alert, to keep order if an altercation breaks out.

The bailiffs have searched every bag and waved handheld metal detectors up and down every single individual entering the gallery that morning—a very unusual move for this normally sleepy, suburban court.

But Judge Whelan believes there is good reason to be cautious.

The federal investigation involving a client of Stephen Bergsten, Jessica's father, is ongoing, and the court has received a tip that Stephen, who is under enormous stress, might be planning to try to physically harm Mark today—the man who brutally raped and murdered his daughter.

Hence the beefed-up security and highly charged atmosphere.

It is against this backdrop that Judge Whelan gavels the sentencing hearing to order.

"I understand, counsel, that both sides have reached an agreement?"

San Diego deputy district attorney Gregory Walden, boyishly handsome, with dusty blond hair and the decorous demeanor of an Eagle Scout, rises and nods.

"We have, Your Honor. Given the defendant's guilty plea, the state has agreed to drop its filing of special circumstances."

Mark visibly sighs with relief. He may very well still die in prison, but at least it won't be by execution.

"We hereby request, however," Walden continues, "that the defendant be given the maximum allowable sentence for his crimes: six years for forcible rape, plus twenty-five years to life for first-degree murder, to be served consecutively, without the possibility of parole."

Jimenez rises to respond—and ask for leniency. He requests that the judge consider running Mark's sentences concurrently, *with* the possibility of parole.

Then he adds, "When my client has the opportunity to give his statement, I urge the court to take note of his remorse and consider showing even greater mercy."

Stoically, Judge Whelan moves on to this next phase of the proceedings.

A hush falls over the courtroom as Mark stands alone and faces forward.

Three bailiffs subtly move into position, standing between him and Stephen Bergsten, who is sitting just a few yards to Mark's rear.

His hands cuffed behind his back, Mark speaks slowly and solemnly.

"Your Honor...God has changed me. And it was no typical jailhouse conversion. I've only gotten but a glimpse of the Bergsten family's sorrow, I'm sure. I sincerely hope that they can accept my apology for my carelessness."

Mark takes a moment to collect himself, and then continues.

"I'm sorry to Jessica. No one deserves to have a dearly loved one taken. I never wanted Jessica to die. And I am...deeply sorry."

Mark hangs his head and sits.

He avoids looking backward at Stephen, but everyone in the courtroom can sense the white-hot rage radiating off the victim's father.

"Carelessness?!" Stephen exclaims, leaping to his feet when it's his turn to speak. "That monster is apologizing for his *carelessness*?! He is a child murderer and child rapist. He is evil incarnate!"

Beet red and trembling, Stephen is just getting warmed up.

He goes on to deliver a fiery, impassioned monologue that lasts over twenty minutes.

"Cowards die a thousand times...and he will die

a thousand deaths! He raped her and raped her and raped her...and then thought, *Let's kill her!*"

Nearing the end of his oration, Stephen starts getting choked up, his wrath displaced by a bottomless sorrow.

"We...We couldn't say good-bye to Jessica... because that *filth* left her," her father manages. "Left her for the coyotes and the goddamn birds to eat her."

Stephen wipes his eyes and nose.

"He says he's undergone a religious conversion? Judge, you must have heard that same story a hundred times. If he underwent a religious conversion, it was to evil, degradation, filth, and satanism!"

The courtroom murmurs with emotion as Stephen takes his seat.

Even Mark, so cool and collected throughout most of the hearing, flicks away a tear as it rolls down his cheek.

It barely seems to register with Mark when Judge Whelan announces his sentence.

Perhaps Mark is already at peace with whatever it is, having faith he'll get the punishment he deserves.

Either in this life or the next.

EPILOGUE

December 10, 2019

THIRTY-ONE YEARS TO LIFE.

That was the sentence Mark Rogowski was given by the court. By his calculation, that means he can expect to be locked up here at Donovan State Prison in rural, southern San Diego County until at least 2023.

True, he was given the possibility of parole. But thus far, that possibility has seemed increasingly remote. Mark's petition has been rejected by the state parole board not once but twice. First in 2011, and again in 2016.

Today, he's hoping the third time's the charm.

Shackled and dressed in the same style of navy-blue prisoner's jumpsuit he wore at his initial sentencing, Mark is led into the conference room by a skinny, baby-faced corrections officer. The CO looks to be in his mid-twenties—around the same age Mark was when he was first incarcerated.

Mark is now fifty-three. Wrinkles and crow's feet line his once youthful, handsome face. He's lost most of the hair on his crown; what's left is closely shaved and largely gray. He's grown a neatly trimmed gray beard as well. Compared to his appearance during his bad-boy fashion model days, he's barely recognizable.

But the biggest difference in Mark's appearance is how he carries himself.

Gone is his manic energy. His wild jumpiness. The rebellious exuberance that made "Gator" the poster child of vert skateboarding counterculture for years.

In his middle age, Mark has become contemplative. Quiet. Almost monkish.

He shuffles to the table and quietly takes his seat across from the stern-faced parole board members: two men, one woman.

"Good morning, inmate Rogowski," intones the official sitting in the middle.

"Good morning, sir," Mark answers respectfully.

"I'd like to start by reminding you of the purpose of today's preliminary hearing. This panel has been convened to review your parole request and make a recommendation to the full California state board. They will have 120 days to finalize a decision. If they approve your request, your case will go to the governor's office. He will have thirty days to review the decision—and if he chooses to, he can reverse it. Do you understand?"

"Yes, sir."

"All right. Let's begin."

For the next half hour, the board questions Mark about his crime, his feelings toward it, his experiences in prison, and his plans for the future if he's paroled.

Mark reiterates that he takes full and sole responsibility for assaulting, raping, and murdering Jessica Bergsten. He expresses vast remorse for his actions, and feels bottomless sympathy for the pain he has inflicted on her family.

"I'm disgusted with what I did," he says somberly.

"I think about it every day. I took everything from that poor family. They have every right to be angry with me. I want to make it go away, but I can't."

Mark then explains how, over the past twenty-seven years he's spent behind bars—more than half his entire life—he has tried to learn from his mistakes and grow as a person. He's earned a bachelor's degree. Taken vocational courses. Become a certified paralegal. He has also continued studying scripture, while supplementing his religious readings with self-help literature.

He says that above all, he has developed much greater control over his emotions. He feels far less anger and has much more patience. A lot less hate and way more love.

In short, Mark argues to the panel, he is a completely changed man, ready to be granted release and prepared to become a contributing member of society again.

The parole board members listen attentively yet impassively to Mark's words. They nod occasionally. Scribble notes. Once their questioning is complete, they lean in and briefly confer with one another.

Mark holds his breath. Shuts his eyes. And prays.

As he waits to hear their decision, he considers the unbelievable twists and turns that brought him to this point. From a life of fame and glory on the half-pipe, to nearly losing his life in a drunken accident, to giving it fully to Jesus, to callously taking another.

"Inmate Rogowski, it is the recommendation of this panel that your petition for parole... be approved... and sent to the full state board for review. Good luck to you."

After so many years behind bars spent reflecting on his former fame and glory, regretting his literal and figurative great fall, contemplating his terrible crimes, and begging for forgiveness, today Mark is one step closer to freedom. To being given a second chance.

Whether or not he deserves it, however, is a question that Mark knows can be answered only by God.

Or by Gavin Newsom. Four months later, in April 2020, California governor Newsom reverses the parole board's decision, denying Mark Rogowski parole and citing his continued "unreasonable danger to society" and need to gain "a deeper understanding" of his crime.

Mark remains in prison, awaiting his next parole eligibility. And still praying for the second chance he never gave to Jessica Bergsten.

ABOUT THE AUTHORS

James Patterson is the world's bestselling author and most trusted storyteller. He has created many enduring fictional characters and series, including Alex Cross, the Women's Murder Club, Michael Bennett, Maximum Ride, Middle School, and I Funny. Among his notable literary collaborations are *The President Is Missing,* with President Bill Clinton, and the Max Einstein series, produced in partnership with the Albert Einstein estate. Patterson's writing career is characterized by a single mission: to prove that there is no such thing as a person who "doesn't like to read," only people who haven't found the right book. He's given over three million books to schoolkids and the military, donated more than seventy million dollars to support education, and endowed over five thousand college scholarships for teachers. For his prodigious imagination and championship of literacy in America, Patterson was awarded the 2019 National Humanities Medal. The National Book Foundation presented him with the Literarian Award for Outstanding Service to the American Literary Community, and he is also the recipient of an Edgar Award and nine Emmy Awards. He lives in Florida with his family.

Andrew Bourelle is the author of the novel *Heavy Metal* and coauthor with James Patterson of *Texas Ranger.* His short stories have been published widely in literary magazines and fiction anthologies, including *The Best American Mystery Stories*.

Max DiLallo is a novelist, playwright, and screenwriter. He lives in Los Angeles.

For a complete list of books by

JAMES PATTERSON

VISIT
JamesPatterson.com

Follow James Patterson on Facebook
@JamesPatterson

Follow James Patterson on Twitter
@JP_Books

Follow James Patterson on Instagram
@jamespattersonbooks